IMAGEOUT*Write*

2012

A Celebration of GLBTQ Writing

Edited by

Gregory Gerard
KaeLyn Rich

Contents

Introduction

In its 2012 season, ImageOut celebrates 20 years of bringing entertaining and educational movies to Rochester. We've enjoyed fine GLBTQ cinema as we've viewed the results of so many efforts: actors memorizing scripts; directors planning shots; crews building sets; producers funding the enterprise.

Enjoying the end product from our theater seats, popcorn and soda in hand, it's easy to forget one of the most important components of the artistic process. We sometimes forget that, before the actor showed up for the audition, before the crew set up the first camera, before the producer and director shook hands—first, there was the *writer*. Someone whose imagination sparked; someone whose courage and determination drove them to pick up their pad and pen (or laptop, or iPad, or…you get the idea!) and create life and art and drama, where nothing had existed before.

It is GLBTQ writers that we celebrate in the following pages. They are the talent behind the talent, the biographers of our time, whose passionate ideas weave the fabric of our stories into the written word. From concepts as diverse as a little boy pope whose papal thrown is constructed of mayapple blossoms—to a little girl angel whose hair exposes a town's ugly secret, this collection provides glimpses into the shared experiences and creative musings of the wordsmiths among us.

Reading their poems and prose, you'll be reminded why, in addition to the actor, the director, the crew, and the producer, it is first the writer that has attracted us to ImageOut again and again over the last 20 years...and it is the writer who will bear witness to our collective culture into the years to come.

--Gregory Gerard, Editor, 2012

Jonathan Everitt

Jonathan Everitt's poetry and flash fiction have most recently been published in *Lake Affect* magazine, *Escape Into Life* magazine, and *Upstate Gardener's Journal*. A freelance writer for both news media and the advertising industry, he also serves on the Board of Directors of the Rochester-based poetry press, BOA Editions, Ltd. Jonathan lives in Webster with his partner of 15 years.

cathedral

before all the whitewashed chapels
there was first a house of worship in the woods

oak arches soaring toward each other
beneath a cerulean ceiling

an emerald-carpeted Vatican
filled with the harmony of wild things

creatures, creeping, flying, darting
through the spongy pews of fallen timber

holy water, poured from white velvet and thunder,
to scent the earth and polish the improbable pulpit

where a little boy pope
would stop, would wonder

before there was a god—
and before there was no longer

a rope swing with a scrap-lumber seat, his papal throne
a slope of low mayapple blossoms, his frankincense

surely less than doctrinaire
but more than any theologian could know

communion down a gravel country road
that would one day carry a little prince

from heaven
to earth
to hell
to home

David-Matthew Barnes

David-Matthew Barnes is the award-winning bestselling author of the novels *Accidents Never Happen*, *Ambrosia*, *The Jetsetters*, *Mesmerized*, *Swimming to Chicago*, and *Wonderland*. He wrote and directed the independent film *Frozen Stars* (starring Lana Parrilla of ABC's *Once Upon a Time*), which received worldwide distribution. He is the screenwriter of the upcoming horror film *Scare Me, Kill Me* and the writer and director of the indie film *Made From Scratch*. He is the author of over forty stage plays that have been produced in three languages in eight countries. His literary work has been featured in over one hundred publications. He is a member of the faculty of the MFA Writing Program at Spalding University.

Latin Freestyle

I remember the rhythm at night:

    Your hips wanting mine,
to grind our street-smart
lust into the crush of summer
heat. The beat of lives
never fulfilled. In the dark you say,
    "Keep it on
the *QT*, *down low*. Slow, go slow.
Just like that, baby. Yeah." I say,
    "When you hit it,
I'm yours *siempre, chulo*."

Our love is different during the day:

The tattooed thug boys
in the park with their sparks,
ankle holsters, packing. They pick
up on the bad girls with halter
tops, hair spray, razor tongues.
I get sliced with fear as you present
me to your neighborhood, your
surrogate *familia*. They suspect

      the whole affair is a white
joke. I try to laugh off their eyes, claims
of their tongue and territory. I sip from
a stolen bottle of O.E., aware I'm out
      of my element, zone. My intrusion
is forgotten when I share a common love

      for the music bumpin' from your sound
system. It makes us dance at Southside, makes us
forget about zip codes, colors, rivals. Makes us pound
and throb like the concrete threat of imagined guns
to our heads, knives to our throats. We know that
when the song is over, we will bleed

for each other. Slowly.

The Day I Almost Ran Away with Goldie Hawn

Maybe because it's Mother's Day
or because we're thirteen and nothing
matters more than bringing home flowers
to the woman who birthed you. After all,
it's what you're supposed to do. But we couldn't
care less about them: mine is an eternal
force of *groundation*; my best friend Karen
avoids hers at all costs, paying
the non-refundable price with her hope. Daisies
we clutch in our hands, the weak petals hit
the sidewalk, white tears to later lead us
back to domestic insanity. We stumble
onto the set of *Protocol*, walk into a shot
where we find something bigger than Sundays
or spring or the crushes we taste on our cherry
stained snow cone lips. Her smile melts me.
She sees us but eyes the flowers. At once, we know
who she is: our real mother has come back and we
are ready to go with her. We always have been.
She reaches and her touch is as soft as a woman's
touch is supposed to be. She palms our faces, smoothes
out the invisible desperation smothering our skin.
We give her our stems and blooms because of the light
in her eyes that tells us she understands. Even though
we are young, we already know:
she deserves the flowers so much more.

In Spite Of It All

In Loving Memory of Dorothy Helen Nickle

My mother tried to make us all feel
better by buying Thanksgiving dinner from Boston
Market, despite her misplaced memories. They floated
around the hospital room in Torrance when my brother

and I arrived from Chicago. I tripped over
my accidental past when reminded there was
a room at another hospital down the street, I'd been
born in: a misfit to teenage parents. We nearly drowned

in my mother's agony; a daughter's deep
grief for her mother, mugged now by morphine: drip,
drip, dripping and digging its sick fingers into us. Later,
in the chapel, I tore from the Book of Matthew, swore

my grandmother should be spared. Begged
for my mother to know I loved her, in spite
of it all. My grandmother, wracked with cancer,
poisoned by years, tears, infidelities, the lack of

affection that can flood one's blood. I touch the silk
of her hair and recall knitted shawls,
the silly verses of *Mack The Knife*, sliced
hot dogs, Gulden's mustard and Eskimo Pies. Piano

vamps and Yves St. Laurent jumpsuits. *The Sonny
and Cher* show. Our living room performances.
The melody of her laughter, pure and sweet. Once,
she said, "I dare you to dream the wildest of dreams."

Over my childhood, tea and soap operas, she made me
take a solemn vow that someday:

I, too, shall see Paris.

Tony Leuzzi

Tony Leuzzi, an Associate Professor of English at Monroe Community College, is the author of three books of poetry, including *Radiant Losses* (New Sins Press 2010) and *Fake Book* (Anything Anymore Anywhere Press UK 2011). In fall 2012, BOA Editions released *Passwords Primeval*, Leuzzi's collection of 20 interviews with leading American poets. His new poetry chapbook--*40, 000 Crows*--was issued by Hank's Original Loose Gravel Press earlier this year.

from "Autumn Leaves"

1

All my life I have felt like that boy, you know, the one who says he will climb the elm to its thickest point and from a screen of foliate green spy on everyone below, as if he were a god gazing on his minions undetected, only when he does it is late October and the leaves begin falling.

2

Every afternoon the boy would wait for his mother's return, whereupon entering she would drop her purse by the door, inhale and sigh, "I'm taking a nap." The moment she laid her head against the armrest of the sofa he would stand behind her, lift it gently in one hand, and with a brush in the other, straighten the frayed strands of her hair. His friends met in the fields and hurled fallen hickories back in their trees, but it never occurred to him that his hours with her were sacrifice. Nor did he imagine she might wish to be alone now and then, free of all touch, limpid, unburdened.

3

Birds appear frequently in my poems, not because I am
enamored of flight or entranced by the power of song, not
even because I am fascinated (though I am) with their
delicate ferocity (such terrible beaks!) but because the
terseness of "bird" can be uttered with a tart clarity I
admire in the chime of bells. Feathers echo.

4

When the priest finished telling a group of students from
the parish what they needed to know about God, he
permitted each a question. A boy in back, wafer thin, with
calm eyes and violent hair, waited until the others had
spoken, then asked, "Is Good more powerful than Evil?"
"Yes," the priest blurted—too quickly—and instantly
grieved the subtle but palpable falling away of his poise,
for he could see from the slight tilt of the boy's head that
he was forming other questions, ones he would someday
answer himself, in rooms more troubled and darker than
this.

5

Each day the boy was taunted by the one he loved. Fairy,
he was called, Cocksucker, Ben Dover, Nancy, Helene.
But the boy heard Fair One, Suck Me, I Will Bend to One
Knee. The heat of words transformed sustained him, and
kept aflame the wick of his longing. Only sometimes, at
night, lying naked underneath his bed, he let the feathery
touch of hands lift him far above houses, the tallest of
trees; and in the clouds he heard two cool sopranos
singing something wordless in unison, and then the
sensuous pluck of a harp, then another. Later, clothed
and sprawled on his mattress, he would recall those
voices, and know precisely what they were.

6

An idea seized me like wind, stilled me like a hand.

7

The date started awkwardly enough, for, despite their mutual attraction, neither knew how to engage the other. In silence they wondered, stirred coffee, and now and then saw themselves slightly distorted in the glass of tall windows. But when two policemen at a nearby table began to criticize legislation favoring same sex marriages, the young men locked eyes and, though still silent, relished in the sudden ease of knowing later promised them kisses and laughter, a drawing of curtains, the removal of clothes...

Brad Craddock

Brad Craddock teaches creative writing at the School of the Arts in Rochester, NY, and is the author of the comic novels *Alice's Misadventures Underground* and *The Curse of the Dark Woods*. His writing has been published in a variety of magazines including *Prairie Margins* and *Zen Bow*. He has had various plays staged and produced, including *Pink Ribbons*, featured in Geva Theater's Young Playwrights Festival in 2002. Currently, he writes film reviews for ImageOut and serves on the Board of Directors.

sharing space

The iconic faces of gold and silver trophies on my
   brother's shelf
never caught my reflection.

A record setter, he outplayed all others in his league
winning the platinum pressed attention of my parents
who spent their weekends cheering him from the sidelines
while I faded, as if by magic, into the deaf leaves of
   paperback novels.

When our grandmother came to live with us I was tossed
   into his room,
his hall of fame, a proud and privileged place, the perfect
   adolescent trophy case.

A tin box on his dresser held trophies of another kind.
My grandfather's wedding ring, my father's dog tags.

In the off season his football jersey returned, smelling
    unfamiliar, a distant whisper
of patchouli and secret flowers, a foreign thing folded
    neatly on his bed.
It told secrets of commitment that I wouldn't experience
    first hand until after college.
How sincere a sixteen-year-olds 'I love you' sounds!

Where was my voice then to say those words?

My brother kept his love notes folded in the top drawer of
    our desk
so that every time I opened it fumbling for a sharpener or
    stapler,
I was reminded of the paper shag that was my own
    loneliness.

On the backs of school pictures, the blue inked praise of
    teenage girls,
the i's drawn round with raw hearts red-hot with first loves,
huddled into corners between white and virgin spaces.

I wondered to what use a strip of Trojans hidden
    underneath it all could mean to me.
In the borrowed pages of his slick sports magazines that I
    hid under my bed

as carefully laid clues to our differences, I masturbated,
incanting the magic words to reshape my flesh to bulk
    and harden like his.

I hated my brother more with each touch down
for how our private spaces intercepted in that place.

Morning Glory

When the phone rings, you aren't prepared. You are cutting flowers, the ones that grow wild outside around the porch. They are purple and don't have a strong fragrance. You can't remember their proper name. You think they may be weeds of some sort, but against your better judgment, you cut them with your clippers and cram them into that vase your aunt bought you at the home decorator's expo. You are trimming them when the phone rings.

He's on the line. You know it's him because his voice reminds you of Alex Trebek. You expect to answer him in the form of a question. He asks if you are there and for a moment you're not sure. You glance around the room and try to find some excuse to get back to whatever it was you were doing to fill the time before dinner.

Oh. It's you. You say.

You want to sound reassuring, no need to let him know you aren't interested in talking. That would be rude. You wonder why he doesn't just text you.

He doesn't notice that you are distracted, which is why you're not sure a call from him does you any good. You pick a piece of lint from off the arm of the couch. Get on with it, you think. You want to get back to doing nothing.

He's asking you out on a date. It's not exactly your worst fear, but it comes right before running out of gas in the poor section of Baltimore. He suggests a couple of options, none of which you hear quite right and you ask him to repeat.

He doesn't, but insists, in that way he has that turns you off, that you make a decision. He wants to know if you are free tonight.

What is, not on your life? You think. But without pausing, you mumble an answer. Sure, you say. You're not exactly clear on why.

Great, he says and tells you he'll pick you up at seven. It's a casual date, no need to dress up. You shrug. You weren't going to dress up for him anyway.

As you hang up, part of you accepts the idea of a free meal at a local restaurant. You weren't sure what to cook anyway, since you've run out of pasta and the spinach you have in the crisper has melted into a green slime.

But the other part of you is baffled. Why did you agree to go out with him? You know he's just going to read some mistaken motive in your acceptance like divining some wisdom from a fortuneteller. It's now going to take you more than a little effort to explain to him when the time comes that you aren't the best choice in a single partnership. He'll want to persist and you'll have to say something like: it's not you. It's me.

But it is him. He doesn't make your skin crawl exactly, but he repulses you nonetheless. Too tall, too gangly. There is something in his gait that suggests an awkward teenager. His clothes and hairstyle doesn't fit him. You doubt you would fit him either.

For the next hour and a half, you move from room to room like a zombie in one of those early black-and-white films—the unmemorable ones, the ones where the zombies just shuffle around and creep you out, rather than attacking.

You forget the cut flowers in the vase. You leave them on the sink counter, and never water them. They will catch the irony of being a few inches from an apparatus that produces fresh, cold water with little more than a turn of a knob. The next morning they will look like you feel.

You decide you have the time to masturbate. You think of it as a precaution, making sure nothing intimate happens between the two of you later due to pent up hormones. Afterward you shower and put on clean underwear. You're not sure why you're bothering, just that the activity fills the intervening time. You apply deodorant for the same reason. You draw the line at mascara. He isn't interesting enough for that.

When he arrives, he pulls into your drive and honks his horn. It's just a little toot, to let you know he's arrived, but to you it sounds like he pressed the horn down with both hands and held it there for a few minutes.

You check your reflection in the hallway mirror and wish yourself luck. You lock the front door and wonder what happened to the days when a date parked, got out of the car, and sauntered up the walk to meet you. You feel the pressure of sinus pain along the band of your forehead and wonder if it's too late to reschedule due to a migraine.

It's better to get the whole thing over with, you decide and try to ignore the pang of hunger that pinches your abdomen. He unlocks the door to the car and you slip in.

His car smells like stale cigarettes and you frown slightly, afraid the smell will grow on you like lichen or some sort of flesh-eating bacteria.

He's all smiles. Like he just told a dirty joke. The ride to the restaurant is filled with his report of what he did at the office today. You think he's a programmer for a computer network or technical help coordinator, whatever that entails. You can't quite make sense of it. He's not CEO material, not that you'd want something that stiff and arrogant, but he's no construction worker either.

He asks how your day went and you filter out any description and censor memories by saying it was just fine.

During the awkward pause after his report, you think of some question to ask to keep him talking. You realize there's nothing you want to know about him.

Seen any good movies recently? He asks.

You can't remember the last time you saw a film, even though it was just two days ago, and you liked the film well enough at the time. You vaguely remember going, but decide that the easier answer is just to shake your head and ask, how about you?

He's seen the latest summer blockbusters and proceeds to tell you all about the characters and plots, which get confusing since he summarizes each movie without clear distinction, so you let him talk while staring out the window to watch the city landscape slide by. He just finishes the synopsis of a film you've already seen as you pull into the parking lot of the restaurant.

It's Chinese cuisine, you realize and recall that he told you that on the phone earlier. You had Chinese last night and so are a little disappointed at the venue.

This one has good pork fried rice, but he raves on and on about something called Buddha's Delight. You wonder how the Chinese equated an Indian religious figure with a chef's special. You amuse yourself by thinking about naming a hamburger combo after Jesus. Perhaps the Holy Trinity: consisting of a quarter pounder, large fries and a shake. Which one absolves sins, you wonder.

While waiting for the waitress to take your order, you amuse each other by comparing Chinese horoscopes. He's a cock, and you smirk at the implications until you examine the placemat that reveals you a rat. Anyway, the Chinese agree with you that this date isn't going to bring much luck.

You order number seven for double happiness: the General Tso's chicken. You remark that you wonder who this general was and why you're eating his chicken. This turns out to be a mistake because he knows that General Tso was a military leader during China's greatest civil war, the Taiping Rebellion. Millions of people lost their lives he says around crunching on a shrimp chip.

Turns out Tso was somewhat of a bastard: a cruel leader that reconquered Chinese Turkestan from the Muslims. You listen to him discuss politics until your dinner is served, but you can hardly bring yourself to finish the dish. You poke the fried brown lumps of chicken hidden among red and green peppers and a miniature bonsai of broccoli. You are thinking about the millions of civilian lives lost. History has too many casualties.

He notices your quiet speculation and asks if the dish is too spicy.

Yes, you say. And pour yourself another perfectly tiny cup of tea.

After he finishes his dinner, something with shrimp, something that suits him, you talk about your father's tour of duty in Vietnam. He doesn't know your father. You're not sure why the conversation has moved to something so personal and disturbing.

He fills the time between placing his MasterCard on the tiny brown money tray and the arrival of the fortune cookies talking about his own parents. How they grew apart in their later years, after the children left home. He talks about lying in the adjoining bedroom and listening to their nighttime quarreling, how each fight was punctuated by a caesura of silence and embitterment. He surprises you by wiping a little excess water from his eyes.

You let him choose his fortune first. He will find the wisdom in truth, but only if he stops seeking. You are destined to find happiness with a new love. The meal ends.

On the ride home, you mention next week's film festival at the local art cinema. Quietly, he asks if you'd accompany him. You pause and consider your busy schedule. A song plays on the radio that reminds you of your senior prom. A sense of nostalgia pinkens your cheeks. Awkwardly, you change the subject to tomorrow's weather.

At your house, he turns the car off and you feel chilled. You don't want to protest or make a scene, you've already rehearsed the right line in your head, but he opens the driver side door without further comment.

You both walk to your door. Gnats and moths swarm around the porch light.

They mistake the bulb for the moon, he says.

Don't we all, you respond.

Good night, he says. I've had a good time.

You've placed your key into the lock and given it a sharp turn.

Me too, you say. Thanks.

He looms above you, blocking the light from the porch for a moment.

Here it comes, you think.

You are surprised when he simply hugs you. You relax your shoulders and allow the intimate moment. His aftershave reminds you of your father. He releases you and turns to go.

Hey, you say. I'm free next week.

You're not sure why you're committing to something without checking your calendar. You're not even sure you should be leading him on. There's nothing that you can say you want from this guy. For some reason, you smile.

I'll call you, he says.

Okay, you say. And thanks again.

His gait down the steps is a little lighter as he climbs back into the dark shell of his car.

You watch him pull out before you turn to go in.

His headlights disappear into the confusion of the night, but he toots his horn as he drives off.

Your hand pauses above the light switch inside before you turn off the moon.

You undress in the dark.

You slide your hands down your chest and stomach to your thighs. It's been a long time anyone's touched you intimately.

As your head presses against your pillow, you catch the scent of clean sheets. For a change of pace you plan to plant morning glory along the trellis next year.

Eboni Sade'

Eboni Sade' is a Jersey City, NJ native with a Bachelor of
Arts degree in Communications from Howard University.
She has been published in *This Old House Magazine, St.
Maarten's Guide to Writing Handbook, The Hilltop,
District Chronicles, HU News Service, The Celebrity
Cafe, The Amistad Journal*, and *The Aah Factor*. She is
also a published model and identifies as a lesbian.

Memories of a Love

The thunder roars and lets go of a boisterous lark
As the sky perspires and tears pummel the face of a canvas
Both hitting with such vigorous force
That it is hard to tell one from the other

Heartache glides down each cheek to form a single strand
of ache at the point where HER neck and collarbone blend

The same neck once used as a playground for HER lover's
tongue to suck ferociously
The neck that handled slight pressure while HER breasts
found their home across the thickness of her lover's lips
HER chest heaves as HER soul remains perfectly still

HER thinks of SHE
SHE who generated a fiery storm inside of HER
SHE who demanded the depths of HER soul
SHE who made eye contact with HER feline-eyed opus
and found

Each word left unspoken
Sensitivity disguised under false armor
And an ego that once snarled left to a soft whimper of
ecstasy

HER nature is to console
To see the rainbow after the storm
And learn to dance in sync

Only this time it is different

The rain is reminiscent of SHE
The sensual, nurturing side that protects and heals
anything SHE touches
The SHE that made love grow in a place where HER
never dared to venture

Until then.

And now.

HER is afraid of this nonentity kinda love
SHE is afraid of falling so quickly
Two canvases standing in a sea of uncertainty
Both broken
Both passionate about one another

HER Pisces yearns to find solace in HER Virgo's embrace
As the rain and thunder drown out HER thoughts again...

Mind Play

I rose to inhale her cerebral intellect
Strategically placed kisses on her frontal lobe
Massaged her temples for good measure
I whispered into her labyrinth
Rose Tea oil glistened atop her skin the color of chestnuts
set out to roast upon the morning's sun, twice over
Smoothed the oil over her breasts and thickness
Created a silky shadow on the achromatic walls from the
nightfall's light
Listened intently to her rhythmic breaths
And waited for her depths to expatiate
I internalized her needs and desires
And healed pains and misfortunes
I enveloped her darkest enigmas
And placed them close to mine; never to be spoken of again
Where she became weak, I transferred energy of my own
And where she grew silent, I became her intonation
I prepared my declension to exhale her Medulla

John Yates

John Yates is a nineteen-year-old Cuban male hailing from New York City. He is the recipient of the Posse Scholarship for DePauw University, which is a full tuition leadership scholarship for intercity youth. He utilizes his poetry as a medium for activism. Coming out of the closet when he was sixteen and contracting HIV only two years later catapulted Mr. Yates into activist circles. He has always been passionate about working towards a better community. Poetry is a way for him to express his activist thought in a more eclectic fashion.

Apathy

So I'm sitting in class,
You know the one where you write fancy little poems,
Cuz,
They say
Only the educated can traverse between prose and poetry
And so eloquently
Speak to me
Simply
In a phonetic harmony
That
Dead white men have been made famous for.

But excuse me, for I digress.

So I'm sitting in class,
You know the one where they make you write fancy little
    poems,
And teacher is trying to use the projector
But she doesn't know what she's doing
And the students are idly sitting there

Just sitting there
And I wonder
How wonderfully wonderful it must be
To have the luxury of just sitting there
Doing nothing short of nothing
And thinking you're doing more than enough

Wait, digressing. I apologize.

So I'm sitting in class,
You know the one where you think you write fancy little
    poems
But they're just words conjured up by the phenomena
That is Bic and Xerox paper
Where all we do is regurgitate
Glorified etchings
Of lionized authors
Because the New York Times tells us so.
But I will let you revel
In your imaginary brilliance
As you just sit there

So I'm sitting in class,
But today isn't like other days
No,
Today we listen
Listen, as truth spills from rhythmic lips
Into ears that remain static
Stagnant,
Quiet
Because they are tone deaf
But I can't help but be moved
For you see I've heard this song before
And so I'm dancing and laughing in my chair
My body embracing the orgasmic hum
While they
Still sitting there
Look at ME as if

I'M the village idiot

But they don't know.

They don't know
I just want to wake up to you,
cook for you,
lay with you
make it all about you type love.

They can't hear the tempo
Behind those rumbling New York City trains
That I always used to dance to
In my Washington Heights bustle
Where fire hydrants run rampant
On hot summer days
And I fall asleep to the lullaby that echoes
From the steel barrels of unregistered guns.

Sure they have their stars in the sky
But I come from a city of stars
The sky gazes upon me
Hoping that I will one day
Grace it with a constellation
That captures the curves of my sensations
And the crevices of my most perverse fantasies

They don't know
Of late night picnics
On black tar rooftops
Past the potheads and crack fiends
Cradled on the security of rickety fire escapes
I would pick my place in the cosmos
As we pondered where we would be by morning

I am the manifestation of broken dreams and empty
    promises
Where my mother's hands felt stronger than my father's

And she always smelt of Clorox and Estee Lauder
Where father means nothing more than the sperm donor
Because that's all he really was
Thinking I didn't know the smell of addiction

I was forged in the presence of Aphrodite's grace
And have since searched for her in a man
He took me
And knew all the right spots
I received him
And in a pant
He received me
Pulsing, throbbing,
Hungry for flesh
Thirsty for love
Quivering at his touch
We came
To the conclusion
And I still remember what it tastes like

They don't know
The different ways to spell orgasm
They say it is a sin for a man
To lay with a man
Like he would a woman
A proud sinner
I have slept with death, made love with death
I am walking death
Mark yourselves with red
And I shall pass over

And so I know the poets anguish
And laugh in celebration
Because we are the enlightened few
For I am not the one sitting there
Just sitting there
Waiting for apathy
To wipe my ass.

Lee

Lee is a lifelong writer and resident of Rochester, the
Finger Lakes, and Western New York who generally
refuses to submit to publications but is grateful that an
old friend provided the nudge and the publishers
acknowledge the value of voices seldom heard in the
region. Lee's main literary inspirations have been John
Donne, William Blake, Patrick Califia, and the
surrounding world with its striking, beautiful, and
sometimes jarring experiences that lead us into ourselves
and unity simultaneously. The red-edged bud in spring,
conversations with strangers, crushing betrayals, kisses
in dank alleys, unexpected camaraderie, neglected
laundry, unshakable internal truths, and the glimmer on
a crow's wings. Poetry is a way of finding those places and
releasing or memorializing the events that led to them.
Lee would like to thank the reader, committee, and the
inspirations for letting this voice be released into the
world.

Rising

My grandfather let everyone believe
he was Puerto Rican and had sight.
He was never a blind native mick.

My daddy was slender with boyish
Aryan looks but the mobsters accepted his blond
and blue and Italian nickname.

His parents remained nameless.

You can guess whatever you want
about my gender.

My sex.
My education.
My whole background, at that.

Just hire me.
Let my work speak.
Please.
What I know is I get you off.
Angrily or happily.
Intellectually,
Physically,
Emotionally,
Spiritually.
Most of all, convivially.
And it might scare you.
If it changes your world,
you might be shocked.

But my job is just
To get
You
Off.

To the next place.

You can hate, love, and gossip.
But I look to the sky,
Ask for help,
And I walk.

We intersect, we do
We love, some cheat, we screw.
And no matter the form,
We walk.

And what about the quiet?
There's been abuse and poverty
at times for me.

But more significantly,
there's always been love.
Intersexuallygenderambiguously, I walk.
My suit isn't welcome with tits.
So I cherish the quiet spots
because that is where all live.

Some day we rise.
Not as radical adversaries.
But as beings—alive.
We rise.
We tend life.
We struggle.
We starve under some damn thumb.
But damn it all.
We. RISE.

C major

It's takeable.
Breakable.
He called her it.
Then there was some book.
And you tried to convince me
it was a fine word for me.
But that sneer on your face—
that cold, awful, cloying embrace,
the frigidness and withholding,
anything that ever held me back,
Said CUNT.

And it wasn't a body part
(bless me my degradation).
It was a takeable, breakable,
naïve,
Me.
You tried to justify.
But please,
Fuck me for the ways
I've been dominated
without giving willing exchange.

Service v. Academia

I need a win.

Not for me.
For people who need it—
Deserve it more.

Stagnancy is wearying.
I need that win.
For Earth. For—Someone. Something. Else.

I need results.

Without them
Allathis is
Academic. Pointless.

It's jerking off to a courtroom pinup shot.
The wig and gavel aren't that hot.

Show me the food in the mouth.
The housing secured.
The child in safety.

I need a win.
Because they are we
And we are them.

Robert S. Costic

Robert S. Costic is an attorney and writer. He is translating a collection of German fairy tales by Theodor Storm as well as writing his own collection of original, quirky tales. Raised in rural Missouri, he currently lives with his partner and two cats in Washington, D.C.

Lydia of the Bears

A long time ago a little man lived in constant fear of death. Every day he thought obsessively about the unavoidable prospect of his eventual death. Its finality and eternity was too much for him, and so he tried to distract himself and others by telling jokes and amusing stories. As long as he could keep telling stories, he could keep himself occupied thinking about things other than his demise.

Over time he told so many stories that he became quite good at it, and people all over the large town came to visit his cottage and hear him tell his stories. His closest friends encouraged him to write some of them down and publish them as a book, so he did so, and within time it became a wildly popular. People in particular raved about his story about the woman who saved a drunk and blind paraplegic from a band of Christian terrorists, even though he didn't do anything but curse at her. The little storyteller appreciated the attention and wealth he amassed, because it gave him even more distractions from his powerful fear.

When Lydia, the rich wife of a merchant, read his stories she summoned him to her palace and offered him an enormous amount of money to simply stay with her and tell her charming stories. The man accepted immediately, attracted not only by the money but also by Lydia's charismatic charm. While her husband journeyed on his long business trips, Lydia ate fruit in her sumptuous lounge and listened to the little man tell his funny stories.

This carefree existence lasted for some time, but then Lydia's young daughter became terminally ill, and, as the girl wasted away, Lydia's thoughts turned darker as she contemplated mortality herself. The little man dreaded this, as it brought his own thoughts back to his greatest fear, but to distract them both and to cheer her up he kept telling his stories, and when Lydia insisted on hearing a story about heaven he gave her elaborate descriptions of the place as a wonderful, incredible paradise with everything little girls could possibly want, from lollipops to dolls to flamethrowers and, as the dreaded day approached, he told Lydia about how her daughter would become an angel too beautiful for Earth and be the darling of all the angels in heaven.

And then the little girl died. Although the girl's father couldn't make it back home in time, Lydia, the little man, and all the servants were there by her bedside as she expired. Bit by bit, like a butterfly coming out of a cocoon, the girl's angel came out of her body, but before she could make it out and float to heaven a hideous gang of thugs barged into the room, muscled their way through the stunned gathering, captured the girl with a giant net, and escaped.

Lydia ran after them, but by the time she reached outside the doors to her palace the gang was too far away. A pedestrian passing by looked at the thugs and looked at Lydia and said, "Did they get your daughter, ma'am?"

She looked at him. "Yes! Who are they?"

"They do that from time to time. They're taking her to the pasta factory. They keep the angels there to make angel hair pasta – have them locked up in a big pen – shave their hair whenever it grows out."

"What? How is this possible? Why doesn't anyone stop it?"

"It's a big business," the pedestrian said. "Almost everyone here makes money from it one way or another. Your husband, he goes out and sells the angel hair pasta around the country. A lot of other people work at the factory. A lot of people sell it around town. Yeah, there are people who don't particularly like it, but people have to make a living, you know."

"Jesus Christ," Lydia said. "Why didn't I ever hear of this before?" But then she realized the answer to her own question: she had been spending all her time lounging around the palace, eating fruit and hearing the little man tell her amusing stories. Tears rolled up in her beautiful eyes as she thought in a flash of all those wonderful descriptions of heaven and how her daughter would be a treasure among the angels. Her dreams—born by those tales—were robbed by this gang of thugs, and now her daughter would never see heaven.

Lydia vowed to rescue her daughter, her angel, but when she tried to enlist the help of the locals no one would agree to help her. It was humiliating the way people would admit that, yes, what that factory did was terrible, and as they said this they would look into Lydia's beautiful, earnest face and turn red with shame. No one wanted to put his livelihood in danger. No one was brave enough to take on a factory that they all recognized as being so much larger than themselves.

Realizing that the influence of the angel hair factory was too pervasive in her town, Lydia realized that if she were going to seek help she needed to look elsewhere. She assembled a backpack full of supplies to journey out into the woods. Her loyal servants warned her that the woods were dangerous, filled with ferocious bears, but when they said this Lydia only retorted, "Well the bears are probably better than the people here."

She made her journey out of town and went deep into the woods. When night fell she pitched a modest cloth tent, climbed inside, curled under a thin sheet, and fell asleep. When she awoke the next morning she saw the silhouette of a giant bear against the cloth of her tent, and when she peeked out, she saw that she was, in fact, surrounded by bears.

"What are you doing here?" a bear said. "Humans are not allowed in the woods."

"I'm sorry," Lydia said. "Am I bothering you? I'm on a journey and just needed to sleep for the night."

"Where are you going?" another bear asked.

"I'm trying to find help," Lydia said, and she explained why. When she described the loss of her daughter, and how she must now be tied up in that factory, having her head sheared by some thug, tears rolled up in her eyes, and as the bears heard the story and saw her cry they began to cry, too, and blow their big snouts.

"Tell you what," a bear said. "We'll help you, but in return we want a favor from you."

"What is that?" Lydia asked.

"We want to live in the town like everyone else."

"Well, I don't know if I have the power to promise that, but I can help you as much as I can."

The bears sighed. "Well, we can't promise that we'll save your girl, can we? But we can try."

Now, one might think that these bears would simply roll into town and overwhelm the factory employees with the strength that nature granted them, but these bears were a bit more special than that. It happened one weekend night, while most people were off from work, that a large convoy of bears rolled into town on their motorcycles, decked in their leather and rubber suits and bearing machine guns. They easily overtook the few security guards standing watch at the factory, and when they reached the giant pen where all the angels were chained they went to work freeing the angels. The bald angels thanked the bears and flew out to heaven.

When Lydia saw her freed little girl she embraced her. "My little angel! I'm so happy to see you again! I love you so much."

"I love you too, mommy."

"Now go to heaven, okay? I'll see you not too long from now."

"Okay, mommy. I'll be thinking of you." And she flew away.

Now, when the locals heard what happened and saw the bears strutting around town with their motorcycles and machine guns they didn't put up much of a resistance, but at the same time they weren't very welcoming. With the factory devoid of any angels, the townspeople were now all unemployed, and they took their anger out passive-aggressively on the bears. As it

became apparent that the locals wouldn't let the bears
into their bars, wouldn't let them live in any of their
homes, and basically wouldn't even give them the time of
day, the bears wondered how they were going to live
there.

"Lydia," the bears asked, "can you help us."

Yes, she had an idea. She used her immense wealth
to build a new little neighborhood in town that she
dedicated to the bears. There were cottages, restaurants,
bars, and stores full of honey, fish, and berries. And as
she hired a lot of the locals to build this neighborhood she
earned their grudging respect, since at the end of the day
their greatest desire was to make a decent livelihood with
a paying job.

The bears now had a home, and they enjoyed it.
When they weren't enjoying their neighborhood they
were lounging under the Linden trees in the town's many
public parks or along the town's charming river. The
bears contributed to the local economy, and the locals
grew to like the bears and eventually even cherished them
as a niche that gave their town distinction. They put a
bear on their town's coat of arms and even built statues of
bears at the street intersections of the most popular
neighborhoods.

And this continued up to this day. Tourists travel
all over the world to see the town with the bears, and
among those who are adventurous enough some even go
into the bear neighborhood and perhaps catch a drink
with a bear at one of their favorite bars. It's quite a treat.
If you ever make the trip yourself and meet one of these
colorful folks, just make sure you ask about Lydia of the
Bears.

Thomas Warfield

Thomas Warfield has performed on stage, television, film, and in more than 100 cities throughout the world as a singer, dancer, actor, composer, choreographer, director, producer, educator, activist and poet. Mr. Warfield is an assistant professor at the National Technical Institute for the Deaf at RIT, teaches an Identity in Social Science course, and directs the RIT / NTID Dance Company. Mr. Warfield is founder/artistic director of PeaceArt International—a local/global outreach organization utilizing the creative process to foster world peace. His *Global Poem In Praise of Peace* garnered global recognition from composer Leonard Bernstein and Mother Teresa, among others. His first solo album, *Celebrate the Moment* can be found on CDbaby.com and itunes.com.

Of Me Myself

Between the ideal and the real
I question the self of God that is me.
Adrift like gray sand, pulled
from the womb of the sea.
In hope of new form,
each daily birth awaits exhalation
to its self-mothered earth.
I open my eyes to view
what I know
while closing my thoughts
to the all-knowing flow.
Stilled, my revolutionary seed
now incased by society, tradition, and greed.
I can't break it free
from needing its proof.

I forget that it's there
while living sings youth.
But soon when the gray is decidedly cold,
when flirtation with life deceptively told,
I'll kneel to my God, Myself, and My Soul
where nothing is masked
then traded for gold,
And there view the barren of that
that I've lived
my unfulfilled seed
the me that's been hid.
I am all I've thought
all that I've seemed and yet
something more, I hadn't believed.
What lives underneath humanity's floor,
a powerful silent invincible core.
I tearfully touch this agelessing treasure
now that life has faded
for ever.
And what I there find
is hard to pretend
the search for myself was God in the end.
Is that what life is, to journey this place
to find what I've found without finding a trace?
I have no more dreams and need no more thought
I am
the eternal,
it's life that is not.

Deep Blue Rainy Day

And the silence spoke
like a thundered blessing
to our enchanted souls,
searching out
beyond the rain-kissed sun-glow.
The view from here
paints fingers against a sky of nearly
erased blue.
Each one a simple faint shade,
of nature's mysterious choice.
Only we could hear
the clouds unspoken whisperings,
like the soft wave of a dream
turning true as it uncoils.
But strength grows rooted
in the earth's bosomed voice.
Surrendering what we want to who we are
we've uncovered ourselves fragile,
as the soaring windless night.
Even the fade to darkness
takes us both too early
before we've found courage
to paint our fingers on the sky.
"Look there,"
I can still see, still feel, and still know
you are part of my hand,
my fingers, my memory.
A bluer than blue sky.
Here, in our world,
a glimpse of moon,
the slowing of fleeting wishes,
I watch the timeless fading
and won't resist.
Nothing changes me. And
I am changed
chasing the day!

Pauline Smith

Pauline S. Smith received her Master of Arts in Creative Writing from SUNY College at Brockport in 2012 and has a Bachelor of Arts degree in English from William Smith College. While at the College at Brockport, Smith was awarded the Hennelore and William Heyen Prize for Outstanding Prose and an English Department Writing Award for her essay "Mufflers". In her writing, Smith combines her experiences in rural Upstate New York with her love of circus sideshows, freakery and true crime.

Beauty Queen Killer

These are the facts of the case as I know them now:

April 10, 1984. Photographer Christopher Wilder kidnaps sixteen-year-old Dawnette Sue Wilt at gunpoint from a mall in Gary, Indiana. Wilder uses his previous kidnapping victim, Tina Marie Risisco, to help him lure Wilt to his car with promises of a modeling job. The FBI suspects that Wilder has been involved in the deaths of at least seven young, beautiful women from California to Florida, and warnings flash across national television: the "Beauty Queen Killer" should be considered dangerous; Wilder has tortured his past victims, some as young as ten years old; he can appear charming and attractive. Pictures of Wilder's face appear on television and newspapers everywhere.

April 10-11, 1984. Wilder drives to Niagara Falls, staying on the American side, where he and Risisco take pictures in front of the Falls. The pair keeps Wilt tied up in their vehicle during the photo session. The three then travel down the New York State Thruway to the Exit 45 motel near Rochester, New York where they get a room for the evening. The cops become aware of Wilder's location.

April 12, 1984. Knowing that the police are trailing him, Wilder drives around the back roads of Upstate New York. He stabs Dawn Wilt twice in the back and once in the chest and leaves her by the side of a road in Barrington, a small farming town near Penn Yan, populated mostly by poor rural people and Mennonites. A local deliveryman happens upon the gravely injured girl on the side of the road. Wilt immediately identifies Wilder as her kidnapper and the local media goes crazy with warnings to young women: Christopher Wilder should be considered armed, charismatic, and nearby.

Wilder flees to Eastview Mall in Victor, New York, where he lures Beth Dodge, a local woman out of her vehicle, a gold Trans Am. He then orders Dodge at gunpoint back into her car, drives her to a nearby gravel pit and fatally shoots her. He drives the gold Trans Am out of the gravel pit. Risisco follows him in his car to Boston where he puts her on a plane back to California. Risisco immediately contacts police and tells them that Wilder is heading to Canada. APBs are issued to all of New York State.

April 13, 1984: In Colebrook, New Hampshire, two State Police officers recognize Wilder and attempt to arrest him. During a struggle for his gun, Wilder is shot in the heart and dies instantly. Newspaper photographs of the dead man show his legs, clad in cowboy boots and jeans, dangling out of the Trans Am door. The rest of his body is obscured.

These are the facts of my case as I knew them then:

April 12, 1984. I am twelve years old, in the second year of middle school in Phelps, New York and stuck in a two o'clock assembly. I sit on the aisle, close behind the teachers. From years of experience, I know that dark auditoriums can be dangerous places for the unpopular kids, filled with the electric hum of a dog pack on the trail of rabbits. The promise of blood fills the air and the pretty kids smell it in their hindbrains.

The principal drones on, "You will wait inside the building for the school bus this afternoon...never get into a car with anyone we don't know after the bus drops us off...parents will wait outside to take walkers home." Mr. Mackel does not tell us the reason for the sudden assembly and I want to tell him that we had heard this one before. That we are the milk carton generation. We know about Adam Walsh. Know never to take candy from anyone (even at Halloween 'cause there might be razor blades in a piece, no matter how small). We know never to take rides from strangers, especially if they are wearing trench coats or look like they might be "funny."

The first spitball catches me by surprise. Three more hit my hair and hang. I try to dislodge the white chunks without touching them. They are heavy with spit and cling to my fingers.

I glance around, not turning my head or giving any acknowledgement that I have felt the wadded paper hit my head. I do not want to see that Tammy Penny is wadding up another ball of paper and shoving it into her mouth. Tammy thinks that her flipped blonde bangs, freshly-grown boobs and high topped pink Reeboks make her too pretty to get in trouble with the teachers. Mostly, she is right.

I slink down in my seat.

The day of the assembly, I am wearing the "new" spring jacket mom bought at the Salvation Army. It is acid-washed denim and has a Palmetto label exactly like Tammy Penny's (only not nearly as cool since it is from at least two seasons ago). Who knows, maybe it *was* Tammy Penny's coat. Wearing my splotched armor all day, even as I sweat under the thick denim, I think that I can avoid being Tammy's target. She will not yell "Piggy" at a girl wearing the same coat as her. I can hide in the sea of kids wearing the exact same outfits that I am currently sporting, like a zebra avoiding the lions.

Until that first spitball, I think I am right. I am not Piggy today. No one snorts at me or wrinkles their noses. No one asks "What smells?" and points at me. No one says "Piggy smells" as we undress for gym or eat lunch or changes classes. Today I am finally Peggy, not Piggy.

That *thwapping* of the spitball against my ear erases the threads of inner-peace I was finally weaving together. I *am* still just Piggy and Tammy climbs back onto her pedestal once again. Always the beauty queen.

I stay in my seat at the end of the assembly as the other kids jostle towards the door. I believe that I can outwait Tammy and she will be forced to go to some eighth grade class on the second floor of the building where I won't see her again today. But, bullies never obey ringing bells.

She waits in the hallway.

Tammy snorts as she walks up behind me.

April 12, 1984. 6:30 p.m. "Authorities now believe that
Christopher Wilder, the Beauty Queen Killer, may be
hiding in Upstate New York." Tom Brokaw's graveled
voice on the NBC Nightly News startles me and excited
shivers race around my arms and up my back. I am
sitting in my parent's living room watching our two
televisions; the larger floor model has a color picture and
no sound. Stacked on top of its cabinet is a thirteen inch
black-and-white with the sound turned all the way up. I
glance from the top to the bottom television
automatically; we have had this set up for years.

"Wilder stabbed a sixteen year old girl and left her on
the side of a dirt road near Penn Yan, a small farming
town earlier today. He also may be responsible for the
shooting death of a woman from nearby Phelps, New
York. Authorities now believe that Wilder may be
travelling with a young girl who he kidnapped from a
mall in California. They may be in a gold Trans Am stolen
from the woman found shot earlier today. Authorities
warn that Wilder may be seeking young girls near malls
or department stores. He may also be using his young
teenage captive to lure other women. "

Mom leans forward from her chair as a correspondent
traces Wilder's path from Australia to California to
Florida and back to California and then towards New
York. Only one of these places registers as anything but
fantasy-land to us.

Mom and I have the same hair: farm-dirt brown and
bluntly cut around a bowl with Aunt Sally's kitchen
shears. Mom's has a few strands of gray poking out from
underneath as if all the color is slowly ebbing from her
core. Her face is pale from too much time spent inside;
her glasses are the same welfare-brown-and-tan swirl as

mine. Mom and I often share clothes too; I see that she is wearing *my* new Coca-Cola polo today and hope she doesn't burn it with the cigarette that continues growing a precarious ash as she stares at Brokaw.

After the news broadcast ends, Mom steps into the kitchen and stares out the window into the solid blackness. We live in the country among inky black swamps where the night is not cut through with the comfort of cones of streetlights like it is in town.

I go over to stand near her and stare too. I wonder if her thoughts are with that gold Trans Am too.

I know that having two televisions, one with sound and the other with picture, stacked in our living room marks my family as not normal. I know that living in a house made of two trailers nailed together marks me as different. But the thing that deeply divides my sisters and me from the other children at school is our mother: Trudy VanValkenburg does not believe in keeping the truth from her children. Any truth, no matter how grim. At an early age, I learned the facts about death and burial, knew there was no Santa Claus or Easter Bunny and that terrible and random things often happened to perfectly good people.

One of my earliest memories is my mother reading to me from Ann Rule's *The Stranger Beside Me*. My sisters and I: nine, seven and four, listened with rapt attention as Ted Bundy, in the voice of our mother, killed teenage girls and children all over the United States. We listened to him as he was caught, tried and escaped. We did not know that other children did not know the story of Bundy as well as they did Winnie the Pooh or little Laura Ingalls. I remember curling my body into a tighter and tighter ball as Rule described Bundy's murder of a twelve-year-old girl. I think that *I* would know better than to go with Bundy anywhere.

My mother never thought twice about leaving true crime books around the house; books about murder, serial murder, mass murder, unsolved murder, and I began to read them by myself in the fourth grade.

I learned to suspect *everyone*.

I also learned about the dark romance of murderers; the sweet traps they lay out for women; the urge to be famous for something, *anything*, no matter how many people get hurt in the process.

April 12th, 8:00 p.m. My mother sits at the kitchen table reading a book about the "Black Dahlia" murder.

My mind wanders outside of our windows to the road we live on. It is a mud-filled, boot-sucking country lane. But that previously unremarkable lane connects Penn Yan, now the site of Christopher Wilder's latest crime—instead of just sitting there taking up space with the New York State Thruway. I wonder where Wilder is at this moment. Is he sitting outside on the road near my house? Waiting outside in that gold Trans Am for some beautiful girl to leave her house so that he could grab her? Is he hiding outside of my school, only blocks away from where Beth Dodge, the dead Trans Am owner had lived, waiting to grab one of the girls inside? Would he take Tammy Penny?

I imagine that I could be the one to find him; imagine that discovering this new national celebrity near my house could be the thing that takes me out of this shack in the swamp where we have two stacked televisions, where my mother reads about killers but is afraid to go find them. Would that be my ticket out of spitballs and "Piggy"? I think that those girls would be scared tonight, the beautiful ones. They would be the ones to worry that Wilder is lurking outside their doors, on their roads.

I want to find him and save the beautiful girls.

April 13, 8:00 a.m.: My plan is simple: I clean my glasses and put on my best clothes and the Palmetto jacket before leaving the house as usual. I will take the bus to school; after all of the students go into the building I will head off to take up a position at the edge of the road in front of the strip mall (the only mall in town). I hope that Christopher Wilder has stayed in town, looking for a young girl to replace the one he left behind. I am not sure if I want to leave Phelps with him. I think that I might call the police and turn him in and get famous for awhile instead. No one would dare to call me "Piggy" once I am interviewed by Tom Brokaw on national television.

I have a picture of Chris (I imagine that he will tell me to call him Chris once we meet) that I cut out from the front page of the *Finger Lakes Times* in my back pocket. On the school bus, I pull out the picture and trace the lines of his face. I wonder if his hair will be as soft as the newsprint under my fingers. In the black-and-white picture his eyes look hooded and gray, but I imagine them as a sharp blue that can change color in an instant.

Maybe I won't call the police and he will take me along with him on the next leg of his trip.

Three hours later than planned, I am finally sitting outside the strip mall across the street from school. When I arrived at school that morning, with Chris in my pocket, the teachers ushered us quickly from the bus into the school and I went along, like a fish caught in a rapid stream.

In the middle of gym, I slipped back into the locker room, dressed and blended into a lunch line with the sixth grades. No one yelled at me when I sat down at a table with a girl I'd never met before. She sweetly talked to me about her dog and her brother. No one threw spitballs. I realized that these kids do not know me, do not know me as Piggy or Peggy or at all. This is the best lunch I have had in middle school and I am sad that I cannot follow the girl (whose name I now can't even remember) back to sixth grade where I am unknown.

My bus driver, stopping for her lunch break at the Great Wall Chinese restaurant at the mall, does not notice me sitting on the curb nearby. I take the picture out of my back pocket every few minutes to trace the bearded face with my fingers and then carefully fold it back into its hiding place. It starts to sprinkle and my glasses become dotted with tiny water drops and my Palmetto jacket begins to get heavy.

I know that serial killers are often found by the police by accident.

Ted Bundy was arrested after a police officer noticed that he had a headlight out on his VW Beetle. David Berkowitz, the "Son of Sam," got a parking ticket near the scene of one of his murders. I decide to walk down Main Street to find cars with tickets under the wipers then search for the owners.

I find only one car with a parking ticket. It is a small gold-colored sedan parked outside the library. I wait for an hour until an elderly man emerges from the library and drives off in it. Not Chris. I suddenly realize that I am not actually quite sure what a Trans Am looks like and that I am hungry and bored.

The rain gets heavier and I debate whether to go back to school or to go inside one of the Main Street stores.

At that time, the Phelps Library was housed in a small building that had once been a church. I am outside of the stone walls, tracing the lines of each stone, when the rain becomes a downpour and I can't see anymore. I jump into the library as a thunderous boom shakes the sky and lightning zings across the clouds.

The stained-glass windows in the library cast rainbow colors over the white walls and the tiny rooms form catacombs of fiction, non-fiction and children's books. I have never been to this library before and find the scents of must and paper and faint spice exotic and different from the peanut butter-and-jelly smell of the school library. I begin dancing my fingertips over the book jackets in the adult fiction section, waiting for the fog to clear from my glasses so that I can go outside again.

Once my glasses clear, I glance at my watch and am startled to realize that the bus will leave school in ten minutes to take me home.

I take Chris out of my pocket. The paper is wet now and the grays and whites of the print have bled together. I try to rub the paper over his face and it slips off on my fingers, leaving behind a hole. I slide the wet paper back into my pocket.

I run to catch my bus.

April 13, 1984. 6:30 p.m. Tom Brokaw triumphantly announces: "New Hampshire State Police have shot and killed Christopher Wilder. The manhunt is over..."

Mom leans towards the television. I see that her cigarette ash is building dangerously long again and it falls to the floor, burning a black hole in the greenish-yellow carpet. Mom doesn't notice the curl of smoke that puffs up from the floor and I step on the smoke to keep it from burning any more.

It's over.

For the rest of junior high, I am just a girl with bad hair and a bad smell. A girl still called "Piggy" by her classmates. I hate assemblies and get hit with spitballs from Tammy Penny. My Palmetto jacket gets lost on a field trip and I get a new plastic coat without a brand-name label from Ames.

I start to write to Dawnette Wilt through the Penn Yan police. I want her to be my pen pal. I can't finish any of the letters and I stack them in the underwear drawer of my dresser, tucked next to the *Times* article where the edges of Wilder's rubbed-out face start to yellow and curl. Sometimes I go to my room and pull out the dried picture. I smooth out the wrinkles. I study Christopher Wilder's missing face. What color was his hair? His eyes? I can't remember and it makes me sad. Like someone I loved long ago died in a distant fantasyland that I could never picture.

Angel Propps

Angel Propps is a femme leatherdyke who has the honor
of serving as the Women's International Leather Legacy
2012. Angel is a frequently published writer of horror,
erotica, poetry, and literary tales with a Southern Gothic
bent. When not travelling she can be found at home with
her butch dyke partner OB.

Towns/people

The town I grew up in was small, unimpeachably Southern.
Mills dotted the landscape like toadstools. Women under
Bright red Sunday hats and their younger versions peeking
From under smaller pink brims, the heated fervor leaking
From their eyes, transcendent joy on each rapt face
As they refuted sin and evil every unending Sunday.
They always backed up from me so carefully,
Their sharp noses could smell that discontent on me:
Difference, Lustfulness, oh the longing for things unknown,
For the taste of a mouth that was like my own.
I often stayed in the musty scented locker room far too long
Deliberately lingering over my clothes, fumbling with socks
Because that tomboy with the wide hips and cocky walk
Would sometimes stroll out of the shower naked, stomp
Out of the shower and into the echoing spaces inside of me
With her skin flushed and dewed with beads of water and
      heat.
Once a foamy patch of lather rested unnoticed on her ass
      cheek;
I wanted to lick it off, to ask her if I could sit on her lap.
Why, I didn't understand, and there was nobody I could ask.

At fourteen those feelings were beyond my knowledge,

my ability
To recognize but those women, those sharp eyed and
    unkind women
With the hats and the hallelujahs and the high pitched
    amens
Made certain their daughters avoided me.
In nineteen eighty three
Those small towns/people were not kind to those like me.

The Graffiti Read

Hell is for people like you. Those who are...
The letters were done in bright red spray paint
and as I stood there I could not help but feel
accused. Was it the way the sentence just
dangled, or my guilt that made me nervous?
There was no answer to that question. It's
possible the writer ran out of paint
or interest. The result was still the same.

I became frightened, felt violated; like
I was being observed by someone: some
unknown person who would come from around
the corner of Seventh Avenue to
mark me as well with an empty can of
paint. With an unexplained damnation of
me for no reason but to put graffiti

Blood-like on cold grey stone, a too bright cry
against someone the writer left unknown.
I stood there fascinated, feeling like
a sinner standing at the gate of a
church whose keeper decided to go out
without leave. Wondering why nobody
else seemed to notice the emptiness of
that missing description and that failure
to name who it was the writer accused.

Damian Serbu

Damian Serbu, an author of gay speculative fiction, lives in Chicago with his partner where they rent from their two dogs. He is author of The Vampire's Angel series: *The Vampire's Angel*, *The Vampire's Quest*, and coming next spring, *The Vampire's Witch*. His other novels include *Secrets in the Attic* (a coming out ghost story) and, forthcoming this fall, *Dark Sorcerer Threatening*. Come visit him at: www.DamianSerbu.com.

Lake Michigan's Calling

The sailboat sits still in the waters of Lake Michigan with the Chicago skyline illuminated beautifully a couple of miles away. I'm not supposed to come out here at night because it's too dangerous. Dad tells me it's illegal, but I never know whether or not to believe him.

Besides, I'm in college now. Staying in the dorm even though Mom and Dad only live a few blocks from campus. My parents want me to find myself and grow into an adult, complaining about my juvenile language that's unbecoming of our family's status. Fuck that. That's *why* I talk that way. Besides, living in the dorm is fine by me because it gets me out of the house. Still, Dad can't quite let go. Actually, neither one can. They're way controlling. Both want certain rules in force even though on most nights they don't have a clue about my whereabouts.

The compelled me to come out onto it tonight, anyway. No choice, really. It's as if the winds whip through my dorm window carrying messages, usually wanting me to come for a visit. Out here. On the water, away from the pressure, away from the burdens, away from the expectations of being the son of two prominent doctors, engaged to the daughter of a corporate CEO who's worth more than God. All strict, upright members of the Republican Party and all things conservative.

Out here in the boat, my mind clears. All by myself with no one blabbering about doing this or that, no phone calls from an unpleasant girl who intends to spend her life with me, no parents berating me after they find gay websites on my computer. Snoops. Wasn't even porn, just news and stuff. Boy did I take a hit for even being interested in that "topic." Good thing my instructor assigned it for a class. It's not high school anymore, so they couldn't check or yell at my teachers about it.

On the lake I can also dream about men – about being with other men. The fantasies consume me – dreams of those one night stands from Halsted Street whisk me away, force me out of the life of expectations and into one of finding love.

Eventually the morning will come and yank me back to reality and the chemistry lab of the pre-med program. Out here on the water, until then, dreams about the Oscar Wilde novel from my English Lit. class, the course Mom "allowed" me to take for fun to educate me in the high brow ways of my future patients, create the perfect alternative world. She also mentioned that it'd improve my high school level vocabulary. More reason to never use a big word around her. She had no idea it was Queer Lit. She'd freak. I need this outlet, though.

The waves gently slapping against the side of the boat tell me to follow my dreams. Leave the money. Leave the family. Work toward that doctorate in gay literature, because you have to follow your passion.

At these moments of despair, longing, or just plain sadness, he comes. Actually, he visits me on the boat quite a bit, no matter the mood. But he always appears to cheer me up. From my imagination? From the depths below? A god? Ghost? Whatever, he comes. And that's why I'm here.

His form climbs out of the water, at first not quite solid but not quite transparent, more like a liquid. Then he morphs into just another guy my age, except he's always wet. Otherwise he looks like any other teenager in their first or second year of college. I tried to touch him once, desperately wanted to, in fact, but he wouldn't let me. He quickly dove out of the boat and disappeared into the water before my hand could touch him. Told me next time that he didn't want to hurt me.

"Hey Water Boy," I say when he sits opposite me.

He smiles, a wide grin that sends me into giddy euphoria every time. "Hey back at you. I'm glad you came out tonight."

I nod and move closer, without moving too fast or scaring him away again. "Did you come to talk? Anything special on your mind?"

"I don't really have much on my mind anymore."

Questions flooded my mind, the same ones since he had first appeared suddenly in my boat. Scared the shit out of me the first time. But I never ask any of them, afraid to offend him or chase him away. Was he a ghost? Phantom? Sea creature? Spirit? What? Why did he lurk in Lake Michigan, and how many guys did he visit?

"Wish I had less on *my* mind."

He tilted his head and twisted a lock of his hair around his finger. His hair entices me, how it frames his face in a wild mess of brown, wet curls. It goes with his pale skin, his undefined features on that skinny frame. "Well, what's on your mind?" he asks. "Just let it go. Or tell me about it."

"You know already. Just my family. School. All the shit I don't want to deal with. Marriage. Shit, and to a woman."

"Yeah, sucks. I wouldn't want that either."

"I wish I could just run away with you. Come on, please?"

He thought for a moment before answering. "I can't do that to you."

"I don't get it. You come on my boat all the time. Flirt with me. I really like you, you know? Why can't I at least touch you? What's the harm?"

He smiles again. Such a wicked grin. "I like you, too. Lots. I don't visit anyone else anymore, except the old guy that just likes to talk about his life and missing his wife. I feel sorry for him. Otherwise I just wait for you. See? We feel the same. We just can't go further, because then I'd never be able to let you go. It's just the reality. You don't deserve it."

"But I *want* it. Let me make that choice."

He shifts his position, getting down into the boat more and reclining back against the side. Water drips down the side here and there where he touches it, though he still appears pretty solid, just wet. He never responds to my plea. Instead, he says, "You're hot."

My face burns crimson. I hate thinking about my body or the idea that anyone else notices it. "Uh, thanks. If you like fat guys."

He laughs. "You're not fat."

"Not skinny, either."

"Well, I'm no sculpted god. You're damn cute. I love your smile, the dimples. I could hang with you every night. We just can't go farther."

We chat like that for an hour. I fill him in on my classes, my mother's latest rant, avoiding my fiancé for the third straight day, and then my cell phone rings. Shit. Dad.

"I gotta go." I start to get the sail boat ready to move again. "Come with me. Please!"

He had stood up. Then he blows me a kiss. Before he jumps over the side, he runs his hands down the front of his smooth chest, teases at a nipple, then dives one hand into his swimming trunks and plays with himself. My dick gets rock hard, forcing me to resist the enormous temptation to jump on him as he disappears again into the water.

The boat glides smoothly across the lake on this clear, peaceful night. A barge moves along down south, as the skyscrapers get closer and closer. It doesn't take long to dock the boat and walk back toward my dorm. I'm such a dork sometimes, leaving my friend behind just because my Dad calls. Like I'm ten years old. Then, to top it off, I never even listened to the message he left.

Walking through the streets, a homeless guy promises that he won't use any money or anything stupid like food, he just needs a drink. I avoid eye contact, my mind focused only on *him*. His white skin with pearls of water dripping down, and his hand diving into his trunks before he disappeared. Then it struck me. Did he have a name? Water Boy can't be his real name.

Too lost in my revelry, I miss that Jan sits there waiting to pounce. She lurches out of the chair and storms toward me, steam coming out her ears, maybe literally.

"We need to talk. Now." She grabs my hand and spins me around, back into the night and toward her car.

I so don't want to get in it, trapped at her every whim. "No. It's late. I have class tomorrow."

"And a fiancé to take care of now and then, you know. Were you on that fucking boat again? By yourself, and at night? Are you just a complete dumb fuck?"

My foot taps at a stone on the ground. "So why do you want to marry a dumb fuck?" Oops, I answered her question with a question, which will royally piss her off. But seriously, how are you supposed to answer the question about whether or not you're a dumb fuck? *Yeah, I'm a complete dumb fuck. Never knew anyone dumber, really. Complete head-up-the-ass idiot. While we're at it, I'm a fag, too, and would rather screw that ancient fireman over there than stick it in you.*

"Just get in. We need to talk."

"How about just going to the coffee shop over there? It's closer."

Jan slams the Porsche door shut and bleeps the doors locked. She rolls her eyes and walks by me. Seriously, this much contempt for the guy you want to spend the rest of your life with? This is so fucked up.

Guess what we get to discuss? She has desires that I'm not meeting. She needs more from me, especially my time. I can either marry her or the boat, though she never poses that in question form because we both know she wouldn't like the answer. She'll drill me about where I go and what I do. Always thinking there's another woman. She's half right, there's another.

What would Water Boy say if he witnessed this scene right now? Would he still find me cute? Or just finally see the utter lack of guts and a backbone in an asshole with no integrity?

She honks away at me without needing a response. I do enough to pretend interest, say a few things to try to appease her, but mostly just wait for this lecture to end.

The phone vibrating in my pants pocket scares the shit out of me. Great, Dad's number lights up the screen. "It's Dad. Gotta take it." I get up and walk outside to the sidewalk and a few paces from the door. Only the need to escape Jan could get me to answer this call.

"Hey Dad."

"I've been calling you all night. Where have you been?"

Nice to hear your voice, too. "With Jan." Oops, I was using both of them now. Him to get away from her, her to stay out of trouble with him. So I possess a manipulative streak? Not bad for a dumb fuck.

"Oh." Works every time. "Well, I worried that you might be out on the boat. Anyway, I called because we need to put it in the dry dock soon. I'll meet you on Friday morning, and we can take it for one last run."

"Cool." Shit. Just two days left until we had to put the boat away. My hands shake as I put the phone back in my pocket and try to gather myself to go back inside.

"What did your Dad want?" Jan asks as I sit opposite her.

"Time to put the boat away."

"Good." She taps her annoying long nails on the table.

"Well, I gotta get up early for class tomorrow. I better go."

"We're on for dinner? I have a reservation at Table Fifty-Two."

Wonderful. A nice long, lovely meal with just the two of us. Planning the wedding and our dismal futures. The dumb fuck and his lovely bride. "Sure."

I get up without waiting for her to follow despite knowing she'll erupt at not being escorted to her car. Thankfully, all her earlier screaming had worn her out so she let me go. My quiet dorm room welcomes me. The darkness provides peace and quiet despite student noise outside my room. Sleep takes me away.

The next morning a raging hard on greets me after a dream of my Water Boy sucking me off. I can hardly keep it down to get to the bathroom. In the shower, eyes closed, visions of the trail of hair leading into his swim trunks provide the perfect erotic fantasy.

I drift through my two morning classes, hardly paying attention to anything that the professor has to say and instead worrying beyond belief that about the mere two days left before Dad yanks the boat out of the water. I wolf down a burger and fries, and then go to my room to wait for my afternoon chemistry lab.

Glancing through my Facebook account proves dull and uninteresting. Who cares that several of my friends went to McDonald's this afternoon? Who cares that you drank yourself into oblivion last night and puked all over the floor? Disgusting. Seriously, I don't really want to know every thought every one of my friends has at every moment.

My pictures give me pause because so many contain the sailboat. Some family friends took one from their boat, so the photograph captures the rainbow sail, the entire length of the boat, and the Chicago skyline in the background. I even like how I look in it, waving and grinning. Out on the lake, nothing else matters. It's safe.

Solitude. The lake calls to me. Slamming the computer shut, grabbing my backpack for the boat, and heading toward the water, nothing else matters at that moment. Even a brief moment close to shore between classes can rejuvenate me.

At least, I intended as much until the sail pulls the boat out of the harbor and onto the open expanse of Lake Michigan. How could I resist another calm and beautiful day, one of the last warm days until fall's chill sets upon the Midwest? Besides, I only have the boat for two more days. Yeah, plenty of lab time remains for this semester, but only two days on the boat.

Not as many people floated around on weekends, offering more peace and quiet. You can find a lot of room between you and other boats or signs of humanity, except Chicago calling from the distance. Far out and by myself, I steady the boat. The water gently laps against the side, and nothing else interrupts the mood. I close my eyes and pretend that I never have to return. Ever.

My groin stirs at the sound of him alongside the boat, tilting it slightly as he pulls himself aboard.

"Sleepy?" he asks.

"Not really. Just content. You?"

"Content." He grins at me, his wet curls again dripping down his cheek and onto his chest. "I never really get sleepy."

"Do you sleep?"

He shakes his head. "Not really."

Another of his vague, strange answers. I never follow up when he says something like that because the mystery intrigues me. Besides, what if I find out something that destroys my image of him? What if he's just another kid on board a sailboat? Someone like me, looking to escape some awful life of straightness? No, preserve his exotic mystery. My Water Boy with his intrigue.

"You look kinda sad." He had sat nearer to me than ever before.

I look over and nod. "Yeah. A bit. Same old, same old. I had this awful conversation with my fiancé last night. She's always pissed I don't spend more time with her, but can't take the hint and just break this thing off. Of course, neither can I because I'm chicken shit. She knows it's all arranged as well as I do. I just don't have the guts to do anything. I'd lose it all, you know? She's sticking around for the money. And the babies. Fuck."

"Rough. You could just leave her, though. Maybe make your own money or something."

He always makes it sound so romantic and easy. But I grew up with all that money and comfort and can't imagine surviving without it, which means without my parents. I have nothing without them. *Nothing*.

"You're cute." Time to divert us to a new topic.

"Afraid to respond, huh? That's cool. I'm just saying, maybe you don't have to play it this way, that's all."

"Can you believe she called me a dumb fuck? Right to my face!"

"She's the dumb fuck. But like I said, strange that you're sticking with it, even with that. Just leave her."

"For what?"

"Me."

That stops me dead in my tracks. He'd never said anything like that before. Never even close. I *would* leave her for a chance with him. "I thought you said we couldn't."

"Couldn't what? Touch? No, not really. Sorry. Marry? Probably not that, either. But hang together? Be here. Just be us. Why not?"

"I'd leave it all behind for you." Leaning toward him, my entire being desperately wants to kiss him.

He pushes himself away and shakes his head. "We can't." He looks sad. "Here. Try this."

He leans over and kisses the side of the boat. "Kiss where I just did."

Confused but grinning, I arch an eyebrow. "Kiss my boat?"

"Yeah." He nods and jerks his head toward the spot before kissing it again. "Come on, try it."

The tingling goes right from my lips, down my spine, and electrifies my groin. I taste the fishy water he left behind but also smell a soft cologne-like odor. A hint of mint, too, as if he just brushed his teeth. I linger there, moaning at the pleasure.

Pulling away and glancing at him, he smiles, his huge, dopey, beautiful smile. There's a bulge in his swimsuit, same as mine.

"Next time, I'll show you even better tricks."

He asks me about class and some other mundane things. I so want to ask about his day, or his past, or something about him. Or get him to show me another trick. He just eludes anything personal.

"Oh yeah." I so don't want to tell him this. "Dad's taking the boat out of the lake, day after tomorrow. Totally sucks."

For the first time ever, he frowns in anger.

"Shit. He can't. What will we do?"

Only desperate answers come to me. "Can you come to the shore? A dock?"

"No." His eyes grow wide, frantic.

"Navy Pier! Can you come to the edge there?"

"No!" Then he cries. The wetness of his form blends with the tears, but his body heaves up and down. Why can't I reach out to comfort him with a touch?

"Hey Water Boy, don't do this. We'll figure it out. I promise."

He looks up and wipes at his tears, though that just left another streak of water on his face from his hand. "Promise?"

"Promise." I nod and kiss the side of the boat. He kisses it back and grows hard again, which makes me excited, too.

Shit, shit, shit. Why on earth does that reminder pop into my head at this moment? Way late for dinner. No way to ditch her again without major fucking trouble.

"Fuck. I gotta go to dinner."

"With Jan? Still up for that charade, huh?"

"I'm just not ready yet. You know? I'm trying."

He nods, back to his laidback self. "So, come back later tonight. I'll show you that trick."

I rub my crotch and wink, and he returns the favor. Then he gracefully dives over the side of the boat and into the water. Where the fuck does he go?

The engine propels me quickly back toward the skyline instead of the slower sailing that anyone would prefer if using the lake for solitude. No time for that today.

Mom always scolds my too-quick-to-panic personality, which causes me to run around like a lunatic out of my mind, stumble, hurt myself, and in the end takes more time after some royally screwed up disaster that a slower, deliberate pace would have avoided. Her control over me pisses me off so much that I can't even listen when she actually has good advice.

So no shock that while hurrying too fast to secure the sailboat after docking it, killing myself to get to a dreaded dinner with my fiancé, splash! The cool waters of Lake Michigan first strike my face, then my neck, and on down my body, right to my toes.

Funny thing, though, is that I almost just stay there despite my ability to swim or grab the side of the boat. I'm not afraid of the water. It's just that the peace and tranquility underneath lulls me into a trance. Kind of like the one when hanging out with Water Boy or dreaming about spending the rest of my life with him. I even wonder what would happen if I just stay under. Would he swim over to me so that we could spend eternity together out in the lake? Was this the answer I always wanted? Maybe.

Some fool jogger on the path near the lake interrupts my contemplation and comes running over to save my ass. He grabs me by the shirt and tugs me up. I thank him, wring myself out a little, and try to calm him down. He keeps wanting to call the cops or a rescue squad. "Chill. Everything's cool. Just a little water."

"But you weren't coming up."

"Yeah, well, that's complicated."

That stops him from babbling more about authorities and checking me out. He just stares into my eyes and nods. "Okay. It's okay." Strange. What the hell did that mean?

"Anyway, I gotta go. I'm late." I jog down the dock, pretending not to freeze my ass off and run as fast as possible back to the dorm.

Thankfully, my phone sat tucked in a

compartment on the boat. No way to listen to the eighty messages that await me from Jan. *Hey Dumb Fuck, where are you?*

Actually, I deserve a gold star. Only about thirty minutes late for dinner with her, when it should easily have been an hour or two. Walking the last couple of blocks to avoid a bunch of sweat in my pits or running down my face, the cooler night air clears my mind before the restaurant comes into view.

Jan sits in the corner, near the front of the restaurant. Cool place, in some old converted house with great décor. Pretty luxurious. Intimate. Too bad the poor fools that sit at the table next to us will hear all this ugliness.

"Hey." I sit opposite her and pretend to smile.

"Hey? You know you're an hour late, right?" She speaks while she pretends to read the menu. The words arch over it and stab me right in the face. Typical. "And all you have to say is hey?"

"It was only thirty minutes. And, uh, people can hear." The woman next to us glances out of the corner of her eye with a stern look despite my whispering.

"I'm sure they want to know you're lame excuse this time, too."

"I fell in the lake."

Her menu flops onto her empty salad plate. She rolls her eyes and then slams her fists onto the table. "Fell in? I'm not a complete imbecile, you know. You would never fall in."

She kind of has a point. It sounds utterly absurd. Except that it really happened. The irony of it makes me laugh. So many past lies about my thoughts, my actions, my behavior, yet I tell her the truth and she goes ape shit on me. Funny.

Of course, laughing doesn't really help the situation. Jan fails to see the humor in it.

I finally convince her of the truth, and she chills out a little. The people next to us stared her into submission, too. We eat quietly, only bickering when the waiter asks if we want any sides and I order the mac and cheese. She thinks it'll make me fat. If fat keeps me away from her, bring two servings. At least the reports of this place's food live up to the billing. Excellent stuff.

Done with the dreadful silence of our dinner, we walk outside. We never talk much except to argue. I don't really know why we ever got ourselves into this position in the first place. We knew each other growing up, our families hang together, and we used to have an okay time. Our parents forced us together, though we made decisions in the whole thing, too. Especially Jan. Anyway, we hardly talk now. Never have fun together.

I *can* explain why I stay in the miserable situation. It's called the closet and an acceptable beard. But what is *she* doing with a dumb fuck?

At her car, I open the door for her, slam it shut, and then lean into the window to say goodbye. It stuns her.

"You're not coming with me? We could go somewhere. Have dessert. Or I could at least give you a ride back to the dorm."

"Nah, it's too nice. I'll walk."

She has that face again, about to erupt like a volcano all over me. So I jog away and wave, smiling back at her. Shockingly, she fails to ram her car into my ass, killing me right there on the spot.

My head a swirl of emotion, I bee-line it for the red

line, not toward downtown and my dorm, but north to the Belmont stop. A two minute walk later, dancing guys surround me having fun, flirting, dancing, and occasionally glancing my way.

What would life be like, out like that? Do they all have families that accept them? Probably not. Just more courage than the pansy sitting here.

The alcohol eases some of my tension. The music and energized scene further calms my nerves. I escape here from time to time to dream about being out and happy. Funny, though, that my drunken stupor doesn't get me out of my seat. It usually loosens my inhibitions and makes me hungry for some yummy boy. We'd sneak off to his place, roll around in bed, suck each other off, and then each plod through some awkward goodbye that night or in the morning. They were never as cute the next day, and no doubt my pudgy body disappointed more than one of them when they really had time to look at it in the daylight. Yet a few wanted my number, so I guiltily wrote some fake numbers on a notecard and handed it to them.

How many potential boyfriends escaped when they dialed and got some old woman, or a business, or the phone company telling them that no such number existed?

Tonight, the more the alcohol takes hold, the more the boat calls to me. Water Boy had promised me something. My groin tingles with anticipation as memories of the passion of kissing the side of the boat where he had put his lips flood my memory.

A cute guy from a few months ago comes over and sits next to me.

"Hey," he says.

"Hey yourself. What's up?"

"Not much. Just dancing. Drinking a little, too."
He tosses his head back laughing, obviously drunk.
"Wanna come with me?"

"Can't tonight. Next time, though."

He pouts out his lower lip. "Not your type
anymore?"

"You're still cute as ever." I pinch his cheek and
laugh. "Positively charming. It's just that I have another
obligation. You go dance your way into someone else's
heart for the evening."

He bows before me and then leans over and plants
a long kiss on my lips, tasting of berry vodka and looking
right into my eyes. He winks as he walks away.

That settles it. He had hardly aroused me at all.
Walking in the chilly night air will take too long, so I wave
down a cab though I hate them, mostly because my
parents expect me to take one all the time. They think it
beneath me to ride around on the El with all the
unwashed masses in Chicago, especially after dark when
they presume that only rapists and murderers ride it.
Translation: they fear black people. Ridiculous. Not to
mention saving the environment with public
transportation. Same reason the fancy car they bought
me sits in their garage all the time. No need for a car in
Chicago. Give me the boat instead.

A sense of urgency and the temperature negate
these ideals tonight. I give the cabbie a twenty for the ten
dollar ride and hustle down the dock toward the boat.
Even with a good buzz, I muster grace and efficiency in
getting it ready to head out, certainly more than my sober
docking of earlier that ended in a lake bath. The engine
sputters to life and pushes the boat farther into Lake

Michigan.

No time for the sail tonight. I just want to get to him.

It takes him a long time to appear. Has he abandoned me? Did he somehow spot me at the bar and sense my moment of near betrayal?

"I've been watching you."

I almost jump out of the boat with fright. Drifting to sleep and waiting, he caught me by surprise with his stealth climb into the boat, sopping wet as usual, and in nothing more than his swim trunks despite the cool temperature.

"Aren't you cold?"

"Naw." He shakes his head and grins, then brushes a lock of hair out of his eyes.

"So you were watching, huh?"

"Ever since you stopped the boat. I just like looking at you sometimes. You're sexy."

My face burns red. I never feel sexy, but somehow he convinces me that he at least really believes it. "So, what've you been up to?" Dumb. He never has anything to tell me.

"Just swimming. How was your dinner date?"

I roll my eyes. "Awful. Shitty. Embarrassing. Need to know anything else?"

"What happened?" He tilts his head, looking so hot and nonchalant. "Did you have to kiss her or something?"

"No!" I laugh. "Just the usual. Well, you already know that I was late. So that pissed her off from the beginning. But it's a pretty small place, so we were close to all these other people. She couldn't bitch at me for too long, or too loudly. Instead we just ate quietly and then left."

"Was she mean again? I'll never be mean to you."

I thrill every time he says something like that. It sounds permanent, like we really have a relationship that will last or something. Funny that I wish for such a thing or think it possible with a boy who lives in the water.

"She was a little mean. She didn't want me eating mac and cheese because it makes me fat."

"You're not fat." He tosses his arms in the air and slaps the sides of his swimsuit in indignation. "Not at all."

"A little." I nod. "Not fat, I guess. Just a little flabby around the middle. I try to exercise and stuff, but I like all these bad foods too much."

"Let me see."

"See what?" The mere thought of showing my skin arouses me.

"Your tummy. Come on." He smiles and pats his. "You see mine all the time."

"Yeah, but yours is hot." I un-tuck my shirt and hold it up. Funny, all this time on the boat with him, all our time together, but never without my t-shirt or wetsuit covering my stomach. Even on the hottest days in the summer I always wear a shirt, too embarrassed to do otherwise.

"Come on, show me more. Lower." He wiggles his eyebrows.

I have to unbutton my pants and pull them down a little to show him the rest of my stomach. He smiles back at me as my hands tremble.

"Delicious. Totally delicious." In one swift motion, he yanks off his trunks and stands naked, his perky penis pointing straight into the air, the bright pink tip winking at me. I so desperately want to wrap my lips around it.

"Let's see yours," he jerks his head at me.

"It's cold."

"Not that bad. Remember, I gotta show you something."

So I undress. What if someone else drifts by? What if the Coast Guard happens to pass and sees me standing by myself, completely naked in this boat? Maybe they could see Water Boy, too. I never wondered about that before.

"Hot. Here, watch this." His little butt walks away from me, over to the mast, and he gyrates against it. Watching his ass muscles contract in and out, up and down, makes me dream of licking down his crack. When he steps aside, he has that awesome, big, dopey grin on his face. "Go ahead."

I march right over to the staff and stick my dick where he had rubbed up and down seconds ago. Without moving a muscle, electricity shoots through my body and sexual passion courses through my every nerve ending. Before you know it, the mast is covered in cum. Wait 'til Dad sees that. On second thought, that demands a good cleaning tonight.

Water Boy sits to my side, jerking himself to completion. He picks up his trunks and twirls them in the air, then sits down, still naked.

"So?" he asks and wipes a spot of cum off the tip of his now tiny penis.

"So what?"

He laughs. "What'd you think? Was it worth it?"

"Uh, yeah. Totally worth it. Wish we hadn't waited so long."

He nods. "Some things are worth the wait."

We sit naked and silent for several minutes before the cold gets to me. "Sorry. I'm cold." My sweatshirt feels especially good right now.

"It's cool." He also puts on his red swimsuit. "What's on your mind? You look sad? Wasn't it good enough?"

I grin and then just as quickly burst into tears. "Plenty good enough. I just wish you'd let me touch you. Kiss you. Feel you. I don't care if I get wet. And I don't want to go back there." My finger directs his attention toward the skyline, brilliant as ever. "Not to Jan. Not to being straight."

He sits quietly while I cry and cry, waiting until the tears subside a bit before he speaks. "You don't have to go back to that world. Ever. You could come out, you know. So what, if you lose Jan? So your parents and she'll be pissed at you? They always are, anyway. Might as well give them a real reason, instead of being pissed just because you're a normal kid trying to find himself. You could do that, you know."

"It's just not in me. I'd lose everything."

"Or gain everything."

"Like what?" I shoot back, defensive and angry. "You? Gain you? You live out in this fucking lake and won't tell me anything about it. You won't let me touch you. Kiss you. That's all I want."

Water Boy scrunches his brow together and frowns. He shakes his head a couple times and then leans far over the boat. He cups a handful of water into the boat and throws it right at me.

I flinch, wondering why I deserve this and expecting to feel the bitter cold. Instead, the warmth of skinny little arms wraps around and holds me tightly. His essence presses against me even though he still sits a few feet away in the boat.

"I know it's fucked up, okay?" He stares right at me. "Totally fucked, okay? It's just, you know, the rules. It can't happen. It is what it is. You don't think I want the same thing? That I'd give anything to be in your arms and sticking my tongue down your throat? I want that as much as you. Believe me, that pole isn't nearly as enticing as that one." He points first to the mast and then right at my crotch. "But all this doesn't justify your suffering back there." Now he jabs a finger toward Chicago. "That's just bullshit. Total fucking bullshit."

He's right, of course, as always. He makes good sense whenever he challenges me. I should come out. With even a small ounce of guts I could stand up to Jan and tell her to go find a different dumb fuck. Next up, Mom and Dad need to hear about their fucking fag of a son. They can either deal with it or write me out of their lives.

The trouble comes with the aftermath. The crying. The disappointment. The guilt they'll throw at me. And, truth be told, the money. Shallow, that. But true. I'd leave behind bundles and bundles of money. No college. No apartment on the Gold Coast. And no boat. No boat, no Water Boy.

I tell him all this again. He stops yelling and just nods his head in understanding.

"Well, we'll talk about it next time some more, okay?" He bites his lower lip. "Next time, okay? Don't go away mad at me."

My stomach churns in turmoil. "I'm not mad at you. I couldn't be mad at you. Believe me. I—" the word chokes off. All the times it mindlessly and untruthfully flew out of my mouth, now this time nothing. Jan's heard it a million times. Why did it stop on my tongue when I really mean it?

"I love you, too," Water Boy says and smiles. God, I do love him.

"Yeah. I love you. Love you a lot."

"Get going, then. So you don't get some dumb chill that keeps you from coming back tomorrow. We've only got one more day."

I nod and start the engine. With my back to him, his soft splash as he dives into the water echoes across the boat.

The next morning, I decide to ditch all my classes again. Only one more day with Water Boy. He won't come to me when Dad and I run the boat for the last time before putting it in storage. The boat skims across the water in record time and out into Lake Michigan.

Water Boy hops on board right away, smiling broadly as usual.

"Ditching class again? What kind of future doctor skips chemistry?"

"One who'd rather be a male whore."

He throws his head back and barks a hard laugh.

"Actually, I came to talk to you about something." My serious tone seems to stop him in his tracks.

"No." He shakes his head back and forth, his lips pressed tightly together. "I won't touch you. We can't."

"Then at least explain it to me. What will happen? Can't I at least have that much?"

He slumps onto the floor of the boat and plays with his toes, probably just to avoid the subject.

Sitting as close to him as possible without touching, his energy radiates from his knee and directly into my very being. "Listen, I don't think—" The words choke me, stopping the rest of the sentence. A freak show plays in my mind despite the thoughts staying deep inside. Needy. Clingy. Emotional. Won't do, since we really haven't known each other that long.

What the hell. He lives in a lake, right? Might as well go all out. "I'm looking at going an entire winter without seeing you. I don't know if I can. Where do you go? Why can't we work something out. Tell me anything, please. It's just hard, you know?"

Tears drip down my cheek. Slumped over, balling, total despair. When I finally venture a glance in his direction, he has tears streaming down his face, too.

"Isn't there anything you can tell me?"

"That I love you, too." He cocks his head to one side and wipes away a tear, which blends into the general wetness of his existence. The fall breeze makes it chilly again today, but he sits in nothing but his swimsuit, as usual, not shivering in the least.

"Yeah. So you've said. And I love you. Desperately, which is really the problem, right? I'm just supposed to let you go until May or whatever, and hope you'll come back when this boat gets back in the water."

"Oh, I'll be back. Right here, waiting. Winters suck, you know."

He deflected all of my questions again, which makes me question everything we have together. Why the mystery? If he really wants to convince me not to touch him, won't he say something to make sure I won't? Like scare the shit out of me or something? *Hey, I'm a dead pirate from years ago, living in oblivion, and touching me will suck you down into the depths of hell. Or, I'm really a slimy ole fish. Or, Satan banished me to the depths of the lake, except in the summer when he forces me to haunt boats. You just weren't afraid, for some fucked up reason*. Anything but nothing.

The silence lingers for a long time. I don't know what to say at this point, but also don't want to lose his company. Silence seems safe. Finally, he breaks the tension.

"I'll make you a deal." He flips his head to get a wet strand of hair out of his eyes. "You said you had to go have lunch with your Mom, right? So you go have lunch. Then come back. I'll have something to tell you then, promise. I'll make it okay somehow. Make it safe for you, so you'll know how much I love you but also why we just can't go any farther. Cool?"

I nod hesitantly. At least he gives me something. "Cool."

To avoid a repeat scene like last night only today with an angry Mom, I dock the boat on time. Back to the dorm, showered, and walking into the restaurant with time to spare, my muscles tense at the sight of Mom waiting in a corner booth.

"Hey Mom." I slip into the booth opposite her and tense even more. She has been crying and has her mouth set in that rigid, overwrought kind of way that means that I've royally pissed her off.

"Would you mind explaining this to me?" she asks without a hello or any other greeting and slides a large manila envelope across the table.

I start to tear the envelope open but Mom reaches across the table and grabs my wrist. First time she's touched me in longer than I can remember.

"Discretely," she whispers and glances around the restaurant, as if spies lurk behind us.

Slowly, I peer into the envelope and gasp at the huge penis staring back at me. Really big. No way my eyes will meet Mom's right now. A few more images mirror the first – naked dudes and penises. Unfortunately, I recognize them all from my last foray onto the internet at home. No explaining this as a class assignment. Shit.

The blood drains from my face and my hand trembles as it pushes the envelope back to the center of the table. Words completely escape me. What does my mother intend by bringing these to me?

"Is this the kind of thing you engage in at college? No wonder your grades suffer."

I roll my eyes. Straight As last semester hardly counts as suffering. Still I stay quiet, not wanting to initiate conversation.

"I suppose Jan may be interested in your sexual tastes. In case you decide to try to bring them into the marriage chamber."

Not going to take the bait. No way. And what the fuck is a marriage chamber? Just my luck, I have a mother straight out of a Jane Austen novel, like the one I bled through reading a week ago for class. Here sits a woman from the 1800s, with whom I have no idea how to communicate.

And if she worries so much about someone else seeing or hearing us, why the hell meet in a restaurant? I know the answer, of course. We meet here to avoid any emotion. At home, she has to take ownership of me. Admit that she gave birth to me and has some responsibility. Has to admit that I grew up right under her nose, regardless of how little attention she paid to me. Here, in public, we can conduct a business transaction. Just like she sits with a drug company rep. who has decided to take her out for lunch, and she can force her will upon me.

"Are you going to say something?" she finally asks.

My lower lip quivers. "What do you want me to say?"

She throws her napkin onto the table. "Well, I'm sorry would certainly be too trite. And a complete lie, so we won't even try for that. I absolutely don't want to know if you've ever acted on these vile proclivities. Perhaps you should explain how you thought you could conceal this, right on our home computer? Or tell me what you intend to do to fix yourself? What kind of doctor puts himself at risk like this? You must hate your father and me so much."

A fake tear trickles down her cheek. Ever the drama queen. Maybe I should tell her that, yeah, I hate them both. Just as much as myself and my life at this moment. Instead nothing comes out. Does she just want to shame me back into the closet? She has at least done a good job of making me feel like total shit. The only difference between Jan and my mom is that Mom won't stoop to saying dumb fuck. But she thinks it.

"Well? When do you intend to explain this to me? How will we fix it?" she asks again.

I rub my forehead and fight the urge to cry, never wanting to give her the satisfaction. Struggling to even my tone as I stare at the water glass on the table, rather than look into her eyes, I whisper. "I'm gay. It's not like that's a surprise to any of us."

"Another one of your little fads that your father and I must endure, then? Will you be able to grow up before you manage to humiliate us all?"

"Humiliate you?" Now the tears do come, against my will. "All I've ever done is try to satisfy you two. I never did my own stuff. Never had my own thoughts."

The rage builds within me. Never before has such intense fury toward someone so engulfed my being. "I don't even know who I am! I'm just your creation. There is no me inside here." I poke my chest hard.

"No *creation* of mine would do this disgusting stuff." She taps her finger on the envelope.

"Can't you just accept me?"

"Stop slobbering all over the place. People are starting to look. Nothing with which I'm affiliated will partake of such practices. You must have learned these awful things in college. I have no responsibility for you."

"Except that I shot out of you as a fag." The slap across my face stings. Finally, I have an emotion toward my parents. Finally, she gave a better response than disappointment.

Smoothly and quietly I push my chair back and stand up, never looking at her again as I turn and leave the restaurant, knowing that she will sit there calmly as if we have just picked a tuxedo for me to wear at a pretend wedding. She'll never risk the scene of calling me back to the booth.

I walk all over downtown for a little while, crying and lost. Everyone looks at me like a freak. Must be how all the homeless people feel when I try to casually walk by without looking at them but really glance out of the corner of my eye, thinking they are all a bunch of nut jobs. When my phone rings and my father's number pops up, I dump the phone into the nearest trashcan.

I try going back to my dorm room to check Facebook or send a couple of messages, but to whom? They all think I'm the rich straight kid, heading for medical school and the perfect life. Sending a couple of porno links to my mother at least humors me.

The hammer from my drawer smashes my computer, obliterating it into a million satisfying pieces.

My roommate comes back and stares like I've gone insane. This sends me into peals of laughter. "It's a long story. Tell ya later. I gotta go."

But go where? Storming down the hall to nowhere. Maybe to tell Jan to fuck off, too.

Sometimes I go to the art museum and wander around, admiring the art and getting lost in invented stories to explain the pictures. I especially like going there in the winter and staring at the seascapes or painted boats. But that sounds too pleasant for today. Too normal.

Of course, only one thing offers a calming allure. Or rather, one person. Entity? Water Boy loves me.

On the dock, I get the boat ready and guide it out onto Lake Michigan, loving the breeze that blows into my face and the fresh smell of crisp, clean air. I wave at another boat as it passes, then prepare the sails and go far out into the lake, farther than ever before.

The skyline drifts away, from a vibrant, exciting city to the lost city of Atlantis, and finally into nothing but a remote thought. My father forbade me from going this far. Truth be told, it *is* too dangerous. One bad wave could destroy the sail boat. One barge that misses seeing me could ram into the boat and send it and me to the bottom of Lake Michigan.

But nothing disturbs me out here on this day. Nothing around me but the warm sun defying the chilly fall temperatures. Nothing but the water lapping at the side of the boat. Nothing but fresh air.

Nothing. It consumes my senses in such a wonderful way.

Just as it all borders on getting lonely, Water Boy lifts himself over the side of the boat and smiles.

"You're out pretty far today," he says.

"I needed to get away. My Mom's a bitch."

"So you've said. Tell me about it." Water Boy sits down and props his head in his heads.

I tell the story again, reliving every painful detail. Then we chat about other things, like the coming winter, meeting again in the spring, Water Boy all the while trying to convince me that I can survive it without him. I listen as usual without letting on that this time is different. His words ring hallow. I never let on to my real plan for surviving the winter, or eternity. Don't want Water Boy talking me out of it.

"You're stronger than you think." His wet hair falls into his face again. "Cute. Sexy, even. Smart. And funny as hell. Fuck 'em if they don't get it."

"Yeah, fuck 'em." I look toward Chicago again, glad to see nothing but water. "Well, I better go."

Water Boy nods and stands to make his usual diving exit.

"Wait. One more thing. Can we kiss again? Another kiss would feel good. I mean, you know. I think, well, since I think we're boyfriends. Since we love each other, we should always kiss goodbye."

Water Boy's beautiful eyes spring to life and he smiles. "Even though I'm out here in the lake?"

"Yeah. No matter what. I just want to be with you." Forever.

"Come over. Let's kiss."

Water Boy leans toward the side of the boat to plant a kiss on the wood. At just the right moment, I launch myself and grab around that smooth enticing waist and hang tightly as we both hurl over the side of the boat. At first, Water Boy's eyes go wide with surprise and then with fright.

I expect Water Boy to protest at this point or to try to fight me off. My whole life came with mostly anger directed at me, so I wonder when he'll go ape shit and yell at me.

Instead, shock on his face becomes that familiar, welcoming smile. As we drift toward the bottom of Lake Michigan, Water Boy hugs me back tightly and plants a passionate kiss on my lips.

Christine Noble

A political scientist by training and poet at heart who just happens to be a pan-sexual trans woman, Christine Noble was born in Brockport and raised in Rochester. Her blog, Hand of Ananke (www.handofananke.com) is a mix of social justice essays and random musings. She has self-published two books of poetry, *Ego Codex* and *Drawing Lines*, both of which are available through Amazon. Recently she has returned to the activism of her youth, volunteering for Planned Parenthood and NYPIRG, and working professionally for the latter, as well as the Working Families Party.

Knot Hole

In the early morning
I contemplate it
that place between my legs
feeling it awaken with me
and my thoughts drift elsewhere
Lost sleep still weighs down my eyes
so it is easy not to see my room
but all of them
the men and women
young and old
hard and soft
driving blood to places
I wish it would not
It presses against the sheets
tickling
teasing
tempting
torturing

and it takes more will than I have
to not give in
I want to lie to myself about it
say my hand has a will of its own
but I know that's not true
as I slip it under the sheets
hating myself
and loving it
I am not supposed to enjoy this
I am meant to resent it
every moment
of every day
that it is not what it should be
Every second that I give in
is somehow proof
that I am not really a woman
how else do you explain
taking pleasure
in the body of a man
I bite my lip
as my breathing quickens
before I know it
it is over
and I am left with the evidence
of my own faithlessness
feeling guilt's tug
from competing sources

Homo Androgynous

I love my Sunday NFL
and sauntering in high heels
I played with sis's Barbie dolls
and my own Hot Wheels

I love to watch some action flicks
or now and then rom-coms
I sit playing my D and D
and watch LOLcats eat their NOMs

I was proud of my Cub Scout cap
but wanted that bright green jumper
yes sir when it comes to sex
I surely am a stumper

I appreciate the older men
with chests covered in hairy curls
and still I can appreciate
the nerdy younger girls

I am top and I am bottom
and everything in between
I am something new under the sun
that you've rarely seen

Still I can be just like you
you husbands and you wives
for the one thing we all really want
is to peacefully live our lives

Jessica Cohen

Jessica Cohen is a graduate of SUNY Brockport, where she studied Alcohol and Substance Abuse Counseling, Psychology, and Creative Writing. She has worked with adolescents in a variety of settings, including LGBT youth services, and both residential and outpatient chemical dependency treatment. Jessica has been a board member of GLSEN (Gay, Lesbian & Straight Education Network) Rochester since 2005 and assists in coordinating the Jump-Start Youth Leadership program and Students of Color Organizing. She currently does independent consulting, workshops, and training related to LGBT youth issues and improving school climate. Thank you to Sue Cowell for sharing her stories and wisdom.

The House on Wilmer Street
Fiction based on interview with Sue Cowell

I suppose AIDS is what really brought us together. Lesbians and gay men. People always come together in a crisis, it seems. And it wasn't any different then. You'd have thought AIDS would have torn apart the community and chased us back into the closet. Instead, it bonded us. We created a new family tree out of twigs and limbs, branches sawed off and left by the side of the road, discarded as diseased by the very trees they grew from.

***

What I remember most about that time is the house on
Wilmer Street. It had eight bedrooms, a big porch, and,
at any given time, about a dozen lesbians in residence.
Myself and seven tenants, plus whatever women who
came calling as friends, partners, or in need of shelter.

It was painted gray on the outside, a compromise of those
confusing years, when everything was beautiful and
damned, spirited and dying.

***

Friday and Saturday nights, Wilmer Street emptied out as
everyone headed to the Riverview—the only women's bar
in the city—a little dive with a back patio down by the
Genesee. There was a pool table and music. You could
still light up inside back then and the cigarette smoke
would encircle couples on the dance floor like some
strange fog. It seemed everyone smoked back
then—smoked and drank, especially the new
ones—women just out and needing something to take the
edge off the fear and longing we all knew so well.

Wilmer Street was where everyone ended up after last
call. It was close enough that we could walk home, even
in the winter. Upon stumbling over the threshold, our
frozen skin an excuse to sit by the fire and talk for hours.
Sometimes, I'd wake the morning after (even with a
hangover, I could never sleep past six)...and there would
be slumbering women strewn like confetti everywhere.
Even with eight bedrooms, I would have to quietly make
my way to the front porch. Every weekend, while
everyone else slept, Wilmer Street and I watched the sun
come up together.

***

1986 was a year after the death of Rock Hudson. Around
the same time that Reagan reduced spending on AIDS. A
year before the National March on Washington. But
mostly, I remember 1986 as being the year that Joe died,
and the year Harvey, his big white cat, moved in.

Joe had willed Harvey to me. Even though I told him that
I wasn't that type of lesbian, that really, I preferred dogs
and cats weren't my thing. I tried to reason with him. I
even offered to find a nice traditional lesbian family for
Harvey to go to. But Joe was insistent.

Even on his deathbed, riddled with pain, he could charm
(or guilt) anyone into anything—his big brown eyes just
got larger with time, his body wasting away. He smiled
and tried to bat his eyelashes. Harvey, lying at his feet,
meowed in cue.

I relented. Maybe because he was sick and when he
smiled his lips cracked and bled, even though it was
August. But more likely, it was because Joe was my
family—the first gay person I met back in the seventies
when I moved to Rochester.

He was a nurse at the university where I was a nurse
practitioner. Even in work clothes, he had an aura about
him. I knew he was gay just like I knew my married
cousin James was gay and the grocer at the corner store.

That first month, Joe took me under his wing, even
though it seemed most gays and lesbians in Rochester
kept their distance. He showed me the women's bar and
brought me to the gay community group for the first
time—located in a big brick building on Monroe with a

back door that let people slide in and out without being noticed. Joe was also with me when I signed the papers to the house on Wilmer Street.

The women at the house sometimes gave me grief for it—hanging out with a gay man so much. They handed me pamphlets about the Women's Peace Encampment, trying to pull me back across an invisible line. But a few years later, even the most separatist of my lesbian friends had put aside their protest placards to join the men in this new fight.

***

Joe and I had seen it come—the signs were there, and our work in the university's infectious disease unit gave us witness to the battles before the war. In those early years, everyone felt untouchable. Even for the men, they viewed it as a big city thing—a disease of the gay villages in New York and San Francisco. They felt safe in their distance and there was a resistance to get tested. And by the time it reached Rochester, it was horrible.

I never was afraid for myself—maybe because I was a woman, or maybe because I was a nurse practitioner. I always took universal precautions at home and work. And I think that's my biggest regret—that I assumed Joe did, too.

He got sick in '85 and for a while I think there was some denial on both our parts. He continued to work alongside the men and women caring for local AIDS patients abandoned by their families and the system. I continued to bring beer and pizza on Friday nights and we drank until the sense of death faded just a bit.

When Joe got too sick to work, I took time off to care for
him. He went quickly and even now, I wonder if he
helped death along to spare me (and himself) the awful
process.

He died and Harvey sat next to his head on the pillow
until the funeral home came. He sat there until he was
gone, then hid under the bed for hours, refusing to leave.
When I finally pulled him out, I saw he was sitting on a t-
shirt of Joe's. It clung to his claws as I picked him up. I
held it to my nose and I could smell him on it. I wrapped
it around Harvey and took him to Wilmer Street, the first
male to ever live there.

Drew Payne

Drew Payne is a writer living in London. His work has appeared in *Chroma, Velvet Mafia, Creative Week, Out in the City* and *Nursing Times*. He writes regularly for *Nursing Standard* and *FS* magazines. Sketches he has written have been performed in the *Treason Show*, a Brighton based satirical review show. His website can be found at: www.drew-payne.co.uk.

Queer Boy

The woman in the kiosk didn't even look at Kieran as he paid his seven-fifty and took the ticket from her. Her black hair had fallen across her face and she only spoke to demand money for his ticket. Kieran then joined the very short queue, only four other people in front of him. At five past nine on a weekday morning there was barely anyone else waiting to board the Ferris Wheel, only a noisy family of a mother, father and two excitable young boys. The boys, who both looked under ten, were bouncing around and excitedly talking about their trip on the Ferris Wheel, whereas their parents already looked tired and worn out.

The attendant, only a few years older than Kieran, and with a dark rash creeping up the side of his neck, ushered the family into one of the wheel's gondolas. His voice was thick with a local accent. "Do you want to go into a pod on your own?"

Kieran nodded his reply. He felt too embarrassed

about being there to voice what he wanted to say.

"Wait a moment then," the attendant said.

Once the family was inside their gondola, the boys ran around the confined space with an over-excited energy. The attendant closed the door on them, pushing down the locking handle, and the gondola slid away from the boarding platform. Then the attendant opened the next gondola's door for Kieran, and with his rush of excitement, almost jumped through the open doorway. His heart was beating fast now as the gondola door closed behind him too. This was it. He was alone in the gondola, no one else there. This was certainly it.

The Ferris Wheel stood on the north side of the city's central square, dominating the grey and dull central library behind it, and was the council's pride and joy. It had been built two years ago, as part of the city's bicentenary celebrations and in another attempt to attract visitors there. At the time it had been advertised as only a temporary structure for the year's celebrations. Its white tubular frame fit together like an elaborate meccano model. It had proved such a success that, instead of being taken down as planned, it had stayed, quickly becoming another one of the city's landmarks. Its white metal wheel towered above all the other buildings around. Its gondolas slowly moved around the outside of its curve, rather than dangling beneath it.

Even though the Ferris Wheel dominated the buildings around it, the gondolas were small. Six people could comfortably fit into them. They were octagonal boxes, with glass walls, two narrow benches to sit on, and an entrance on the outside edge, which while locked for the journey around the wheel, had a bright red emergency bar across the middle.

He'd been on the Ferris Wheel once before. His mother had taken him on it as a treat for his previous birthday. He'd loved it, the experience of riding the Ferris Wheel, but especially the view of the city from the three hundred and sixty degrees of the gondola. When it reached the top of its circle, the view had been amazing, almost the whole city lay before him like an elaborate and very detailed model, the trains and cars moving around like model toys themselves. Yet it had ended all too quickly, their gondola returning them to the ground and his mother ushering him out of it. He'd just wanted to go round and round on it all day, admiring the view, but his mother had been meeting Larry and was far too busy to listen to him. At least she'd taken him on the Ferris Wheel, at least she'd give in to that request of his, and he'd have the memory of it etched into his mind.

Now he was returning to the Ferris Wheel but on his own. He hadn't told anyone he was coming here today. He knew if he did someone would have stopped him, report him to his mother, claiming he was too young to ride on his own. He'd played truant from school to come here. He'd nervously hidden in the old garages behind their house so he wasn't seen by his mother and Larry had left for work. Then he'd caught a bus into the city. All throughout his journey, even as he walked up to the Ferris Wheel, he'd expected someone to point at him and call him a truant, shouting that he should be in school, but the small number of people he meet just ignored him. He'd been building up his courage for so long to do this, to steel himself for this big adventure, all the while telling himself he had to do it.

As the gondola pulled away from the boarding platform, beginning its ascent up the circle of the Ferris

Wheel, Kieran felt his body begin to shake with nerves but he couldn't back down now. It was all too late. He pressed himself up against the gondola's wall and watched the view around him, but his mind was racing with too many thoughts now to concentrate on anything.

He hated school, each day he felt a physical dread as he took the bus to school, and this only left him when he was back home in the late afternoon. It wasn't his studies he disliked so much, he actually liked that side of school. What he hated was the other kids he was forced to share his school day with. They were cruel, blunt and unforgiving creatures who seemed to be constantly posturing and fighting for position. He was bottom of this vicious hierarchy, everyone looked down on him and he knew it. The other kids felt free to physically and verbally attack him. He'd be walking down a corridor at school, clinging as closely to walls as he could, when without any warning he'd be kicked or punched by someone passing. The ringleader of his persecution was Wayne Smith and his gang, though he referred to the other boys who followed him as his "homies."

It was Wayne Smith who'd first called him it, but soon everyone was referring to him as "Queer Boy." That was the best option he received, often the name-calling degenerated into vicious homophobia attacks, obscenities and lies screamed at him with such force that he even longed to just be called "Queer Boy." The taunting also carried on in the classroom, but rarely did any of the teachers stop it. They would ignore it when he was called "Queer Boy" during a lesson. They seemed far more interested in keeping order then protecting Kieran.

The bullying didn't stop with the name calling either. On a daily basis, he was licked or punched or spat at because them saw him as gay. Long ago he'd stopped fighting back. If he did, it only made the beatings worse; if he didn't react at all, his tormentors quickly grew tired and moved away, even though Kieran was always cringing inside. He never felt safe. On his journey to school he'd always encounter one or another of his bullies. Even his journey home was filled with danger. Wayne Smith and his gang would often be waiting to take out their frustrations on him with their fists and kicks. Often he'd lay awake at night, worrying about what would happen to him the next day at school.

Just thinking about school made him feel physically sick; he'd do anything not to have to go there. Home might not have been the ideal place but it was far safer than school. But his mother didn't seem interested in his complaints, though he didn't tell her how far the bullying went and certainly not about being called "Queer Boy", which would have caused her to ask too many awkward questions.

The year before at school, Angel Lund, a girl in his class, had been schooled at home. All her lessons were sent home for her and marked days later by their teacher. It was never explained why she was away from school and being treated like this, but Kieran envied her. She'd escaped the daily nightmare of school. She'd been so lucky.

When he asked his mother if he could be home schooled she replied:

"Don't be stupid Kieran. I haven't got the time to waste on your nonsense and I can't give up work so that you can stay at home from school."

When Larry, his stepfather (Kieran refused to call him dad) heard this he'd told Kieran:

"Man-up, you little twat!"

"Man-up" was Larry's sole advice to him, whatever problem Kieran had, even though Larry never explained what he meant by it or how to do it. He seemed to believe that just saying it was enough and that Kieran would automatically know what Larry meant. Kieran didn't but he knew better than to ask Larry. His stepfather was blunt in most things and seemed to believe that all you needed to be a man was to be strong and just to get on with things.

When Larry had heard that Kieran was being bullied at school, he'd snapped at Kieran:

"Fuck's sake Kieran, stand up and show them who you are!"

"I'm Queer Boy," Kieran had silently muttered under his breath, "everyone knows that, so what's the point?"

His mother had met Larry when Kieran was nine, only six months after she'd left Kieran's father. Larry had only recently left the army then, and his sole topic of conversation was his "glorious" life as a soldier (even now, six years later, Larry still had a limited range of conversation, and his favorite subject was still his life in the army). Six months after they met Larry moved into their home, and though he never married Kieran's mother, Larry insisted he was Kieran's "step-dad" now. Kieran had never warmed to the man, he found Larry's simplest take on being a man and macho alien and difficult, but he also knew he was a disappointment to Larry. Larry wanted him to be a tough, macho boy, who lived for sport and the out-door life, and wouldn't take any shit from anyone, the complete opposite of who Kieran really was. He tried to keep away from Larry as much as possible. His mother always took Larry's side in any discussion or argument.

Home was just a place to hide away from school in, no more.

Three weeks ago, Paris Braithwaite and her "posse" had cornered him at school, forcing him back against a wall. Paris Braithwaite considered herself the prettiest and most popular girl in their year at school, and as such she felt it was her right to tell others what she thought of them and what was "wrong" with them, whether that person wanted to hear it or not. Her posse, her three friends with the same hairstyle as her, were always ready to agree with her too.

Paris Braithwaite had pushed her angular face into Kieran's and hissed:

"Me dad says all queers like you should be dead, 'cause you spread disease. So go on, kill yourself and put us out of your misery!"

"Yeah!" Her posse agreed.

Then they had laughed along with Paris Braithwaite, but because he hadn't replied they'd soon moved off, looking for someone else to pick-on. But he'd heard what she said. He probably would be better off dead, at least then all this bullying would be over and he'd be free of his miserable and unhappy life.

The thought kept replaying in his mind over and over in the following weeks. If he killed himself all the pain and torture would be over and he'd finally be free of it. It wasn't as if anyone would miss him or even be very upset if he was gone. His mother saw him as an inconvenience, Larry didn't hide his disappointment in him; school was a nightmare with no friends to help him through it. He was the nobody that nobody cared about, and nobody would shed a tear if he was dead. But if he died at least the pain would finally stop.

It was such an attractive thought. With that began the plans of how he would kill himself. There were no pills at home he could overdose on, Larry didn't believe in painkillers so his mother didn't buy any. Neither had he any access to a gun, and he was too afraid to use a knife on himself, too afraid of the physical pain and not cutting himself deep enough to actually do the job effectively. His mind kept searching for the right method, though.

Two days ago, both Wayne Smith and Paris Braithwaite, with their associated friends, had found his Facebook page. It had been the one place in his life that he'd been able to keep free from the bullying at school, a place where he could hide away from it all, but in only a few hours that was all gone. His Facebook wall was plastered with homophobic comments and threats of violence from Wayne Smith, Paris Braithwaite and their followers, every one of them calling him Queer Boy. He'd sobbed when he saw it. Sobbed at all the hate that had defiled his Facebook page and sobbed at his own stupidity for not turning on the right privacy settings.

The next night, after he'd taken himself off early to bed (Larry had been again complaining because Kieran wasn't interested in playing football), he'd heard his mother and Larry arguing.

"You seen the kid's Facebook page?" Larry demanded.

"We agreed to leave him alone there," his mother replied.

"Have you seen it?" Larry again demanded.

"Yes, of course I have," his mother said.

"Is it true?"

"All that stuff on it about him being queer?" his mother said. "I don't know."

"He better not be queer," Larry snapped.

"He's just different, quiet," his mother said.

"I don't want him queer. I saw queers in the army, fucking disgusting. That's why I left, when they let queers in. I'm fucking not living under the same roof as one."

"He's not queer," his mother told Larry. "He's just different and kids pick on that. If he was queer I'd be the first one to slap it out of him!"

Kieran had crept back into his bedroom at that. Even his mother didn't like him and he thought, out of everyone, she would be the one who should care about him. There was nowhere left to go now, but no one would miss him anyway.

Last night, as he lay awake in bed in the small hours of the morning, the idea had come to him. He didn't need a gun or pills or poison, all he needed was seven-fifty for a trip on the Ferris Wheel. Its gondolas had emergency exits, the red bar across the door, and all he had to do was open it when the gondola was at the top of the wheel. It would be over in seconds.

Aged fifteen and six months, Kieran decided his life was no longer worth living and he now knew how to end it.

The Ferris Wheel was now seconds away from the highest point of its circuit. He could hear his heart beating loudly in his chest but he couldn't stop now. Kieran stepped up to the gondola's door and took hold of the red bar across it. All he had to do was push the door open and then fall through it. He didn't even have to step through it, all he had to do was fall forward and then it all would be over.

Kieran held his breath and pushed down hard on the red bar, but it didn't move. The bar stayed rigidly in place and the door stayed firmly closed. Panic seized his mind and frantically he began to push down and shook at the bar, again and again, but it obstinately stayed in place. His body filled with energy as he violently shook the red bar, but the door still didn't open.

Then an electronic alarm sounded in the gondola. The loud sound bounced off the glass walls and filled the tiny space.

He cried out in frustration as tears suddenly blinded his eyes. He let go of the bar and fell back onto one of the wooden benches there, as his body was taken over by wild sobbing.

Jes Gonzalez

Jes Gonzalez attended the creative writing program at
SUNY Oswego, despite all common sense and parental
advice. She always knew she wanted to write, and
continues to be seen in the cafes of Rochester with a
notebook and headphones. Jes occasionally reads locally
and works odd retail jobs.

Queer Theory

"Not gay as in happy, but queer as in fuck you!"
– anonymous

fuck you
    who are the majority
    who are disgusted by my difference

fuck you
because yes i am queer—
    strange
    abnormal
my sexuality is a fuzzy line
of incongruent attractions
    expressions
    admirations
    attitudes

because my gender is also blurry
at best
the expectations—
    that i only top
    that i only date femmes
    that i only fuck women

are blatantly incorrect

queer means doing what i need
queer means doing what i want
queer means refusing to make arbitrary decisions—
    i fully believe it is better
    to advertise my flexibility
    despite society's inability
    to accept my rejection
    of acceptability

i may change my mind later
i won't get caught in hypocrisy

because attractions shift
like bodies can change

because who says girls can't have mohawks
and who says i'm a girl anyways
because sex is supposed to be about pleasure
and it may or may not be private—
    what i do in my spare time
    has nothing to do with most of the yous
    who choose to assume
    based on a series of visual clues

because i wear cockrings on my wrists
because i fuck with my fists
because it's worth the risk
to feel freely expressed

because i will sit down and write
another line about how much i love to be fucked
by a girl in a harness
and dress
    see—there again
    that incongruentness

because i'm tired of playing by rules
i never agreed to
and try to break in the very act
of kissing another masculine set of lips
savoring the way our mouths meet
and duel for dominance
only to open my teeth—
to suck them in at last

because i find joy
in the surprise of discovery
the ability to think my way
out of the box
and back in it—
    though i make it different
    though i expand it and break it apart

because who's not to say
between last night and today
i won't find a nice boi to lick my boots
before i fuck them

and maybe down the line
i'll be the boi
in a skirt
getting my queer cock sucked

Kim Krenzer

Hall of Shame

Since I'm a textbook narcissist, I've decided to open a museum about the wonder that is me. Imagine my accomplishments, from my first step to college graduation, documented for the world to see! People of all generations can fawn over the awards I've acquired; first prize at the pediatric dentist's office art contest, most improved in algebra, outstanding French vocabulary. *Je suis impressionant.* Fortunately, all documentation of my awkward middle school stage, or "The Pork Chop Years," has burned—I mean, disappeared. Weird, right? Honestly, I'm just so fascinating, it would be a crime not to display myself. The most detailed exhibit will be "The Greatest Loves (and Follies, Through No Fault of My Own) in My Waking, Homosexual Life." Fit that onto a plaque.

We can begin with my trial run in heteronormativity. Oh, my poor high school boyfriend Dave*. So tall, mousy and excruciatingly Catholic. I will feature the ticket stub from that time we saw the god-awful remake of "The Pink Panther." I felt particularly philanthropic that evening and let him have a little boob action. Second base (over the shirt) in the back row of our local, shoddy googolplex. I've always been a classy broad. Our feet stuck awkwardly to the floor, remnants of jujubes and cherry cola coated the bottom of my light green sandals. I tried to be turned on, but just couldn't muster it as dust from the projector cascaded upon us as if an omen from above. In retrospect, my internal, raging lesbianism didn't help either. The next day he called me and apologized for giving into temptation, insisting we hold off until marriage. I told him that I was very sorry, but I'm really, really, really gay. We haven't spoken since.

My favorite section will be dedicated to Carly*. A hospital bracelet from the day we met can lay gingerly in a display case. She is credited as the only girl who ever legitimately made me forget my name. Carly was a ridiculously attractive eleventh grader with flowing, strawberry blonde hair and quite an "endowment" in the chest region. I met her when I was in tenth grade and miraculously skinny as a result from my summer of active intestinal infection. We bumped into each other at the local water fountain. She carried herself like a goddess and I swore her feet never touched the ground. She cordially extended her hand and asked my name; I stammered out two incoherent syllables before slipping on a puddle. Naturally, I had chosen the most dilapidated water apparatus in the entire building. Forever a Good Samaritan, Carly rushed to my aid and her big blue eyes blinded me more than the concussion I sustained. She insisted on riding with me to the hospital. We struck up a hesitant friendship days later; hesitant only because she was afraid of causing me more pain and I because of the tingles from my freshly homosexual libido. Three months later under the wisdom of very illegal wine coolers and truth or dare games behind the bleachers, I confessed the real reason for my concussed noggin. Within seconds, her tongue had found its way down my throat and I was nothing short of proud. Last I heard, she was married at twenty-two and living in Nebraska.

A hidden section will be devoted to the enigma that is Cady*, the bane of my high school existence. All six feet of her. A crinkled, faded piece of paper will lay in a glass case. I probably shouldn't put her phone number on display, but she broke my heart. Whenever she passed me on the way to third period Art History, a wave of jasmine and vanilla attacked my senses. My immature, amorous and ultimately frail psyche was a goner. She wore hippy skirts and lizard-shaped earrings, sang in the vocal jazz ensemble and read Kerouac. She was easily the coolest senior ever. She owned the entire Kerouac anthology and could quote him at the drop of a hat. Her voice had a gravelly coarseness that would make Janis Joplin proud. After a year of me being her lap dog, she told me, on instant messenger, that I couldn't be her girlfriend because she was "involved" with Jack. She said, "My fault, my failure, is not in the passions I have, but my lack of control of them." Whatever.

A rather plain portion of the exhibit will include my ex-girlfriend Alyssa*. On a plaque, I'll mount the sticky lip gloss I wore the last time we kissed. She was attractive and dark-haired, opinionated and independent. She taught sexual equality to her peers. She loved Jeff Buckley and Rufus Wainwright. I had no reason not to like her. She giggled when Faith Hill's "This Kiss" came on the radio while we made out in her car. Our break up was quite congenial.

I'm obliged to include a small section for my best friend and former roommate, Rhona*. I've seen her naked enough times that she gets in by default. I've also seen her throw up more times than any human being ever should. Once, while I was being intimate with a girlfriend, she ran into my bedroom, stole said girlfriend's clothes, threw them down the stairs, high-fived me and frolicked away. I cannot make that shit up. As you can imagine, that girlfriend and I didn't last. But, she was a total bitch. Rhona is the perfect dating filter and the dearest friend I've ever had.

The real meat of the exhibit hinges upon my one, true love. I mean, after fifteen-year-old me got over tepid heartbreak by a cold-blooded whore (it's possible that I carry a grudge). My late teens and early twenties have been steadfastly dedicated to Elizabeth*. You can take this time to imagine me as a naval officer, standing still in a crisp salute on a fast-sinking ship. She holds at least half of my heart. Which is generous, considering that I have two parents, four siblings, and intense feelings of loyalty to Gwen Stefani, despite her solo career. Elizabeth is easily the sweetest, kindest, most benevolent person I've ever known who has not one bit of her shit together. I've spent years pining; waiting for her to realize what great spouse material I am. We've grazed by respective failed relationships, zigged, zagged. Hell, we've even tap-danced, but we never forgotten how much we mean to each other. However, I recently came to the realization that it will probably never be in the way I'd hoped. Her section will be darkly lit.

I'll include a collage of the various college girlfriends that hated me. Some of them didn't even attempt to like me. Women who could only speak to me in a condescending tone. Women who started planning (read: *controlling*) our wedding and children after a week. Women who hated my habits, but couldn't give me a good reason for it. All while I've longed for the woman who will love me unconditionally.

By the end of the tour, you will be able to find me sitting somberly at the end of the hallway, contemplating how it's come to this. On second thought, perhaps I won't open up a museum. I don't think I can avoid the inevitable quarter life crisis at seeing my flaws and failures explicitly displayed to the world. Here I am, at the cusp of twenty-three, fearing that my last days will be lived out as a spinster; fifteen or twenty cats as my children. After all, who can love a textbook narcissist, standing in their own way?

*All names have been changed with very little effort for publication purposes.

Eddie Swayze

Eddie Swayze is a poet, performing artist, actor, visual artist, electronic music composer, and educator. He translates his poems into American Sign Language along his original composed electronic music and some videos. He discovered ASL poetry in the 80's through Peter Cook, Debbie Rennie, Clayton Valli, Pat Graybill, and other great ASL poets/performers.

His poetry has been published in *The HandType Press, The Gallaudet University Press, The Clevis Press, The Tactile Mind Press, Dark Lady Press, The Talon Magazine, Forge, Science Poetry* from Ontario, Canada, *Silver Blades*, and more. His poetry performance is featured in a short clip in "The Heart of The Hydrogen Jukebox" by Miriam Lerner. He received two New York State Council on the Arts grants and four Strategic Opportunity Stipends grants.

Rainbow Wings

For thousands of years,
They hid in cocoons.
Couldn't spread their wings.
Couldn't even fly.

Slept in the dark
Like cities without sun,
Dormant without dreams,
Ice-cold for years.
Snow hugged their cocoons.

They pushed their walls
Though difficult to do.

Some ripped them
But too few.
Some slipped into the light
But cruel society mocked them.
They slipped back into their cocoons.

Then one summer year,
They had enough.
They ripped their cocoons into shreds.
Threw stones and bottles. Set the streets on fire.
Flapped their wings in rainbows and
Blew cruelty away.

Years came by,
Many cocoons thawed and opened.
Many of them spread their wings and ascended into the air.
They tasted freedom, the delicious fruits, and
Savored them all, sweet with great boon.

Yet they looked back over their shoulders and
Remembered the others
Who couldn't come out.
They pondered upon sheer suffering,
Then turned their heads back in front of themselves and
Dreamed for the better.

They flapped their rainbow wings through the societies
Though hard work against great challenges.
They twisted the nuts and bolts to play
However nasty the tasks had to be.
They refused to surrender,
For they wished upon the better for the future generations.
They painted the rainbows on the future generations' wings
And said, "Shall your wings flap stronger in brighter
rainbows for many years to come."

Kiss Him For Me

My wishful dream
Popped alive
Like pink champagne bubbles.
They floated wild upon the air,
Tingling my scalp beneath my hair.
I looked at a fine sculptured dude
And became mesmerized by his sheer beauty:
The way he stood, the way his eyes glistened,
The way he smiled,
In all that bursted my heart into bubbles.
Yet to seethe for a kiss
Became too hard to buy
When romance didn't arise.
In a mirror, standing in front of me,
He was embedded in the reflective glass.

In my fantasy, I could walk into the mirror
And explore him deep and through
Yet the glass became solid and barred my way.
Nothing could take me, take me, take me in.
I said, "Kiss him for me. I'll find another one later."

I'm laughing at the champagne bubbles floating around,
A total nonsense, all in pink,
Too far from the reality.
It's just a tease for no good in the blue.
A new party dream shall flow into another day or night
Where possibilities could arise.
I shall dance away and head forwardly.
Again, I said to the mirror where this distant dude stood,
"Kiss him for me. I'll find another one later.
Kiss him for me! Kiss him for me!"

Fire

Boot up!
Gaze into the photon lights and open the
program. Dive into the metaverse, then you see a glowing
avatar: lovely and handsome, dressed in a neon-blue
three-piece suit with perfect groomed plastic black hair
and precise wedge-shaped plastic face. He's standing on
the steel street. Bright acid violet beams glow along the
streets. Blade-gray sky looms thick above him. Look at
that young dude. Gorgeous as heaven, isn't he? Oooh,
ahhh! Look at how he stands in his pair of neat black
shoes. Oooh, ahhh! See how his v-shaped torso entices
your eyes powerfully. Soon he notices you; his silicon
neon-blue eyes allure you. You can feel it; he's sucking
you toward him, an electronic vampire. You're standing
so close to him.
"Would you like to go out with me tonight?" he
asks you.
You say, "Oh, yeah."
He walks toward a three-dimensional black box.
Pink Avant Garde font type neon light blinks on and off
on top. It reads "Pink Flamingos".
The man's activated cracking voice flirts with
you, "I love your smile!"
You smile back with your gleeful eyes. Oooh,
ahhh! Look at his 3-D-rendered baby face. Oooh, ahhh!
Look at his digitized watermelon-shaped butt. Oooh,
ahhh! See how it snuggles into his blue pants: perfect,
smooth, and nicely firm. You and the lad enter the black
box. Inside it's a cyber nightclub.
"Hey, it's party time! It's party time!" he says.
Many half nude sexy men shake their firm asses
on the pulsating electronic floor, flirtatious and suave.
Oooh, ahhh! Look at their muscles twitching and
contracting. Oooh, ahhh! They turn you on into fire!
The man softly whispers into your ear, "Ready to

dance?"

You say, "Yeah."

He guides you to the dancing floor, and begins to wriggle and writhe. You start along, flirting back with your eyes. My God, my God, my God, my God, I'm going crazy! Move it! Don't stop! Oooh, ahhh! His ass flexes neatly. Oooh, ahhh! His arms flail in the air sexually. He unbuttons his shirt and magic explodes from his plastic chest. Look how it glows: smooth marble-white, smooth milky-white. You shake like a wild artificial peacock. Shake your highlighted colorful feathers skillfully! Move it! Groove it! Dance into rave! Rave into it! Rave into the techno trance! See how all the men move their bodies? See how he moves his body? Move your body just like their bodies! Oooh, ahhh! Sweat it out! Oooh, ahhh! Pump it out! Sweat covers your flesh like plastic sheets and plastic mask. Sweat trickles down on his sculptured chest and it glistens in the flashing lights. Sooth it! Smear it! Feel it! The sweat don't bother you, sexy like some hot melting wax. Wax it up! Whip it good! Shake it up! Shoot it real quick! You and the man palpitate, penetrate, pump and pump, and lock and lick into each other.

Your heart repeats into rapid gigabyte rhythms: fire, fire, fire, fire, fire, fire, fire, fire: hair-to-hair, bones-to-bones, and blood-to-blood. He licks your neck, vampire-like, and you scream in ecstasy. Oooh, ahhh! Feel his butt contract as he penetrates you over and over and over and over. Oooh, ahhh! See his whole muscles compress majestically again, again, again, again. God! God! God! God! You want more, more, more, more. Hot red lava spews up in the air! Hot red wine spills all over! Hot red humming birds flutter their wings! Hot red gas sizzles all through your body! Explode like a Big Bang, Big Bang, Big Bang, Big Bang! Yes! Yes! Yes! Yes! Your heart ignites into fire, fire, fire, fire, fire, fire, fire, fire!

Shut down!

Shauna Marie O'Toole

Shauna O'Toole is a former physical scientist and science teacher who is restarting her life after transitioning. She is an author and public speaker about her journey. Her books in print include: *You Can't Shave in a Minimart Bathroom*, *My Transition Checklist* and *Recycled*. All are available at Lulu.com and Amazon.com. She is the proud parent of two incredible children who love their Trans parent very much.

The Attack of the Killer Geese:

a Children's Story

I awoke with a start out of a deep, dreamless sleep. It took a moment to remember where I was.

It was a beautiful September day. The kids were playing in the yard and I had spent this autumn day raking leaves. With the job complete, I sat down to rest and enjoy the afternoon sun. The chair was just too comfortable and, soon, I had drifted off.

The kids were pointing at the sky and shouting to each other. That's when I saw them. Geese. Their honking has caused me to wake in a cold sweat for over twenty years, and probably will for the rest of my life.

My youngest one, Liam, saw me staring at the sky. He came running over and jumped onto my lap.

"Daddy, would you tell me about the geese again?"

"Sure," I replied with a forced smile. "A long time ago, back when I was a little boy…"

It was a cloudy afternoon. My sister, Beth, was drawing another sketch. I was finishing another video. It was a typical lazy Saturday. Mom called to us and said that we had some left over bread that was going stale and asked if we wanted to feed the birds.

"I know!" Beth said. "Let's go down to the lake and feed the geese!"

The movie was over and I knew Mom was chasing us outside to play. The sun was starting to come out from behind the clouds, so I said sure. We ran outside to wait for mom by the car. Beth had her drawing pad and I was humming the music from some action movie.

I didn't know that it was going to be dangerous.

Mom dropped us off near the lake and said she would be back soon to pick us up. There was a family of ducks near the water's edge. They looked hungry, so we thought we should give them something to eat.

We tossed a few bread crumbs in their direction and the ducks pounced on those first scraps. Beth threw a few more crumbs into the water so everyone could have a nibble. When we stopped the free meal, the ducks came out of the water and quacked for more. A few last crumbs sent them back into the lake.

We didn't know it, but we were being watched very carefully.

There was a flock of geese a little farther down the shore. We walked over to feed the closest group of birds.

Like before, we threw some bread crusts out into

the water. The geese attacked the crumbs as if it was their first meal in days. They pushed and nipped at each other. Feathers were flying everywhere. The rest of the flock looked at us. Waiting.

They were hungry, too.

We threw some more crusts into the water. It was enough to feed a few more geese, but not enough for everyone. The geese started coming out of the water towards us, honking and hissing as they came.

I started to back away slowly, throwing crumbs in their direction the whole time. More geese came over to see what was happening. They saw the bread and started honking and hissing for their share. Soon, geese from all over the beach started to close in on us.

My imagination was starting to run wild. I swear that I could almost hear theme music in the background. It was the sort of music you hear when the bad guys come on the screen.

The geese almost seemed to be saying, "Drop the bread, and no one will get hurt."

We were outnumbered, and it wasn't looking good for us.

I suddenly bumped into something. Someone. It was my sister! She had been backing away from her own flock of angry geese. Now, here we were, standing back to back, facing more geese than what we could count.

I had seen this happen before in the movies. The heroes always ended up protecting each other. It always looked fun and exciting. Well, it was exciting, but I was too scared to be having any fun. Besides, didn't one of the heroes usually die in this scene?

"These geese are a lot bigger than the ducks," Beth said.

"Yeah, a lot bigger!"

By now, there were geese all around us. They were honking for bread and all I had left were a few slices.

"Beth," I whispered. "I'm running out of food!"

"So am I," she whispered back. Beth looked up and down the road that ran by the shore. "I wish Mom would get here!"

We threw a few more precious bits of bread at the flock. A few geese in the back slowed down just long enough to grab the morsels, but it didn't stop them. They kept coming right at us.

Closer.

And *closer*!

The movie music was getting louder in my head

I remembered hearing in school that birds might be related to dinosaurs, maybe meat-eating ones. I started to wonder what these dino-geese were going to nibble on first. I decided that I would make good finger sandwiches.

"I'm scared!" I whispered. "What are we going to do?"

It looked like there were more geese than ever! Now some seagulls and the first family of ducks we fed wanted to come to the feast. I wasn't sure there would be anything left for them after the dino-geese finished having us for dinner.

"We're not going to make it, are we." It was a statement and not a question. All sorts of movie scenes were racing through my head now. None of them pleasant and all of them involving the dino-geese that had us surrounded.

Before Beth could answer, our rescue pulled into view. Mom was coming down the road. All we had to do was get to the car without being eaten alive.

Easier said than done.

"Listen, I have an idea," Beth finally said. "Give me the bread."

I looked down at the single piece of bread I held in my hands. Just one tiny bit of crust to keep a zillion geese from eating us alive. I whispered back the only thing I could think of.

"Are you *crazy? No way!*"

"Trust me," she said confidently.

There was something in how my sister spoke that made me trust her. I handed her my last scrap of bread and held up my hands to show the geese that I was out of food. That seemed to make them angrier.

I was sure going to miss my fingers.

"When I shout 'now,' I want you to run for the car," she said. "Don't look back, just run. Okay?"

My whole body shook in reply.

Mom's car was slowing to a stop. The geese paid no attention to it as they continued their relentless match toward us.

"*Ready...*"

Mom honked and waved at us. The sound just added to the feeding frenzy.

"*Set...*"

We were doomed, and Mom couldn't stop it.

"*...NOW!*"

Beth threw the last crust at the flock and then *charged* at the birds. I mean she ran *right at them!*

There were feathers and wings flying everywhere. Honks, hisses and shouts filled the air. The movie music was reaching its climax!

"*Run!*" I heard her cry out.

She didn't need to tell me again! My legs were like bolts of lightning. In a flash I was in the car. I nearly slammed the door on a goose that still wanted a piece of me. Probably a finger.

As the cloud of dust and feathers started to settle, I looked for Beth. I couldn't see her. The geese were probably eating her alive while I sat in the car! I had to rescue her!

I was just about to jump out of the car when the other door suddenly opened. My sister calmly climbed in and fastened her seat belt. There were a few feathers on her, but she seemed okay.

"Did you have a good time?" Mom asked.

"It was okay," Beth replied. "The geese were a little hungry."

"It looked like it," was all Mom said.

I looked at Beth and she at me. Then she gave me a wink to know that everything was fine.

Then I did something I had never done before. I reached over and took my sister's hand. She gave it a gentle squeeze and smiled at me. I smiled back in relief.

She was the hero. I was the sidekick. And I was okay with that.

I looked up from telling my story and saw that the rest of the kids had gathered to hear it as well.

"I like that story," Liam said, and ran off to play.

I smiled and was about to get up...

... when I heard *them!*

I turned and there was a gaggle of geese sitting on the lawn. They were between me and the back door of the house.

They started to honk angrily. The geese almost

seemed to be saying, "Drop the bread, and no one will get hurt."

I could hear the movie music starting to play in my mind...

Georgia Beers

Georgia Beers was born and raised in upstate New York and has been writing for as long as she can remember. She has written eight novels to date and has won a Lambda Literary Award, four Golden Crown Literary Society awards, and the Gold Medal for LGBT Book of the Year from ForeWord Reviews in 2012. She lives in Rochester with her partner of eighteen years, their teenage niece, two dogs, and a cat. For more info, check out www.georgiabeers.com.

Insignificant

Five beautiful syllables, that's what the word is. You let it roll around on your tongue like an ice cube or the maraschino cherry from a sweet and tangy cocktail. It tastes good in your mouth. It feels even better to your soul.

Insignificant.

It's been such a long time coming. Such a long, hard, excruciating time. You've been through hell...worse hell than you ever thought existed. The kind of hell where demons await you at every turn...where they surprise you when you least expect it...where they surprise you even when you *do* expect it, and you're sure their sole purpose is to tear the skin from your body, rip the sanity from your head, one horrifying strip at a time. It's like being trapped in a deep well of endless black, clawing your way up the filthy, stone-covered, slippery sides towards that tiny dot of light far, so far above your head. And in that moment, that one split second when you start to think, "I can do this. I can make it," there are those demons, their talons reaching you, tearing at your clothes, your hair, your skin, until you lose the tenuous grip you had and you fall back down, down into the dark to start all over again, certain you'll never, ever escape.

That was your life for what, a year? A year and a half? Wallowing, clawing, crawling, struggling. And then it happened. The next step finally came.

You got mad.

Not just mad. Furious. Outraged. Royally pissed off. Who the hell did she think she was? Where the hell did she get off treating you like that? Like garbage. Like dog shit. What gave her the right to take the years you invested together and throw them away like used tissue or old socks? Of course, thinking about all the time you put in only made you sad and miss her more, but that was okay. You didn't know it at the time, but you were making progress.

Anger was progress.

Who knew?

Insignificant.

You strove toward the word. Stretched. Reached. Wished.

Instead of avoiding the anger, instead of trying to ignore it, you turned toward it. Into it. You embraced it, felt it, let it in, let it rip through you. You yelled and screamed. You threw things. You broke things. You saw nothing but red. And flames.

And you *hated* her.

Oh, how you hated her.

You made lists, endless lists. Lists of the lies she told. Lists of the insults she hurled. Lists of the things she took. You had lists all over the house, written in red pen, written in red Sharpie, written in black nail polish. You collected them all. And when the time was right—how weird that you just *knew* when the time was right—you gathered them all, put them in the fireplace, and burned them.

A cleansing by fire.

A white hot farewell.

A rebirth.

And the anger was gone.

Okay, maybe not gone, but it certainly eased up considerably. You realized what a waste of time and energy, what a futile activity it was to be angry. It sucked you dry, took everything you had, but gave nothing in return. You decided simply that was enough.

You'd had enough.

She took enough.

You gave enough.

Enough.

You didn't know it at the time, but you were making progress.

Letting the anger go was progress.

You were lonely. There was no denying that, and loneliness is not fun. You discovered the best way to combat the loneliness was to stay occupied. So, you busied yourself. You found hobbies. You took lessons on a pottery wheel. You volunteered at a homeless shelter. You wrote poetry. And you felt good.

Every lump of clay that became a crooked vase or an ugly plate or a lopsided bowl chased away the loneliness. Each poem, no matter how childish or unbalanced or just awful, energized you. Every homeless person who favored you with a smile filled you with love and pride. And soon, it didn't matter that you were alone because you were no longer lonely. You were eager and strong and happy. Hard to believe, but you were happy.

And this time, you *did* realize it. You were making progress. Creativity was progress. Philanthropy was progress.

You weren't certain, though, that you'd reached the finish line because we're never certain until we have proof. Human nature rarely allows us such confidence. So you agree to meet your friends at a local hang-out, and you don't dwell on the question that's lurking in the dark recesses of your brain: will *she* be there? You shut the door on it and don't allow yourself to worry, instead checking your look in the mirror, surprised at the satisfaction on the face reflected back.

You arrive, your friends are there, and the evening is a good one. You laugh, you joke, you drink. Eventually, one of your compadres points out an attractive blonde. She's in the corner with two others and, as your friend informs you with a grin, she's been checking you out all night. The suggestion is made that you buy her a drink.

It's good advice.

You saunter over to the bar and chat up the bartender to ascertain the blonde's drink of choice. You order one to be sent with your compliments. It feels good.

As you turn to head back to your posse, your eye catches on a familiar skin tone, a recognizable earring, and *she* comes briefly into focus. She smiles widely—that same open expression that sucked you in so long ago—and seems about to speak, but you barely notice and keep walking because all your attention is on the blonde. You want to see her face when she gets her drink. You want to raise your beer in salute when she looks your way.

It isn't until later, much later, after you've got the blonde's number in your pocket and you're certain it's scorching your pelvic bone, that your compadre mentions the presence of *her*.

You scan the remaining patrons, of which she is not one, and shrug, truthfully commenting that you barely remember the encounter. That earns you a hearty slap on the back and you're suddenly lighter, unburdened, more relaxed than you can ever recall feeling.

And you immediately understand why.

It's finally happened.

You stand there and absorb it, let it wrap itself around you.

Inhale deeply.

Exhale slowly.

And you grin.

She is insignificant.

You are free.

Susan Jordan

Susan Jordan is an editor for *The Empty Closet*. She lives in Penfield, NY.

Small Talk

No I don't want to have a nice
day or a great
weekend it's just
a day or weekend
like any other
however
in the sense
that once again the great star
crawls over the curve of the world
the mighty wind roars through
the trees the monarch
butterfly penetrates the flaming
red sunflower
in that sense
yes
I have had a
great
day

Skinchanger

Orlando grows his winter fur
thick & black, I put on
my Onion River coat
my winter pelt, drab khaki
but in the lining
violet hints at more to come

hints at spring to come
as light shuts down the candles flower
your birthday roses drop their petals
quietly as snow

a burning grain ignites
inside the dark
inside our winter hearts
as cold and slow
we turn and shift and sigh
beneath our coats of night

Jon McDonald

Jon McDonald lives in Santa Fe, New Mexico. He has written a satirical novel, *Divas Never Flinch* published by Brighton Publishing, six screenplays, a children's adventure story and cookbook, a humorous vampire tale called *Bloodlines – the Quest*, an ironical political thriller, *The Seed* and numerous short stories collected together and entitled *Snapshots*. He won first prize and was published in the *New Mexican* holiday short story contest, 2009. He has been accepted for publication in *Jonathan* and *Raphael's Village*.

Cry of the Wolf

Note: *I discovered this manuscript during my genealogical research at the* Institute Historique Strasbourg *in 2003. In the ensuing years I have worked diligently to carefully translate this manuscript into English. It has been my aim to capture the natural feel of the original manuscript without updating it or making it sound too contemporary. I will leave the final judgment of that to the reader. However, I feel that this document provides a rare glimpse into a life in the fourteenth century, and an examination of a subject little understood or referenced at that time.*
        --Henry Traubb, Chicago, 2010

Nineteenth of March in the Year of Our Lord 1347

I am Warin, son of Ranulf and Alma of the House of Thann by the town of Arzviller, a day cart ride from Strasbourg on Rhine. I am writing this because I know not what else to do. The sadness in my heart must find some form of expression and I may not speak of my story with anyone. I write this for myself alone and pray that it will never be read by another living soul.

It is late at night. I do not have left but a short candle by which to write. It is quiet in the great house and I can hear only my own breathing, the wind whispering down the chimney, and the cry of the wolf in the far field; or perhaps the nearby Cham Woods. I hear his cry almost every night at this time. He is a lone wolf; his pack long wiped out or moved on. He cries often—hunted, unloved, separated, and no doubt always hungry. He does not seem to wake the neighbors or my family. I alone hear his pain.

I am of two and twenty years. My father is the principal landowner in this county. His serfs raise sheep for wool, and then we weave it in our warehouse and trade it in Strasbourg, shipping it down the river to even greater trade centers.

Our family name is much revered and feared locally. The great Emperor Charlemagne bestowed on our family the crest of Lion Rampant Reguardant above a quadrant shield with two crowns and two fields of stars. My father is very proud of this great honor and finds every occasion to display it prominently.

My mother and my sisters, Nesta and Linota, are modest by comparison to my brash father. They are adept in the womanly arts, and peacefully pursue their quiet lives hidden away from the toils of either village or city life.

My father has engaged me to Celestria of Alcuin, but we have yet to marry at the time this narrative begins. She is dark of hair and pleasing of appearance, and their land adjoins ours and will enlarge our domain greatly. That is very pleasing to my father, who dreams of our lands reaching all the way from the far reaches of Lagarde to the edge of Arzviller. I have met her but twice, and she speaks well, and is adapt at tapestry, I understand. If my report of her seems less than enthusiastic it is because of what has transpired in my life this past year and is, indeed, the subject of this writing.

To begin, let me reflect upon my character and temperament – if one may be objective about such an examination. I have been told I am comely. I am dark of hair and have eyes of blue, a rarity in this region. I ride well, and have learned all the skills necessary to engage in commerce, at my father's insistence. I already manage the warehouse where the wool is prepared and woven into a rough cloth, much desired for its warmth in the mountain regions to the south. I have a slight build and have never excelled at the martial arts, to my father's great disappointment. And though it is a passion with my father, I find the hunting of any animal or bird abhorrent. But it is something I must do, as I am a now a grown man, and am expected to contribute to the family table.

I have a burning passion for books, though they are very rare and difficult to obtain. Our library is scant, but I have been blessed with the opportunity to borrow volumes from the Fathers at the Monastery in Ascenseur. They are very kind and attentive to me, and gladly lend me books for as long as I need them. I sometimes wonder at their kindnesses to me, though. They are so pleased when I visit, and seem greatly reluctant to let me part. I am as yet unschooled in many of the ways of the world, but I believe I can detect longing and sadness in their eyes when I finally depart with my saddlebags tightly packed; with the anticipation of many hours of reading pleasure ahead of me.

I have few friends. I was schooled at home. We live far enough from the village so that I grew up with few boys of my age, or of my class, available for friendship. Those that are on our estate are of serf families and are not considered suitable companions for one of my station. My sisters, while friendly, live in a different world altogether, and our paths rarely cross. Nor do we have enough in common on which to base a friendship. And, I am afraid to say, they are rather dull, being interested only in assembling their trousseaus and obtaining a prestigious marriage.

This is how I see myself—neither a hero, nor a villain. My life is regular, for who I am—and untouched by either great joy or great pain. That is until a year ago, February.

And here I am in the depth of night about to finally commit my story to writing, a lasting history that will forever seal my fate.

I work regularly now, as I have stated, in my family's wool warehouse. It assists my father, and he is pleased with what I have accomplished there, thus far. Besides the keeping of the accounts, I supervise the workers—carding, spinning and weaving the wool that comes from our lands. I then accompany the carts to Strasbourg and oversee the loading of the merchandise onto the barges headed to southern ports, where it is eventually sold.

Not long after I began working at the warehouse, I found myself in need of an assistant. Most of our workers are dull and listless, needing constant prodding and oversight, and I despaired of finding a suitable candidate from among our most uninspiring dullards. However, one lad caught my eye. His name is Sevaric, and about the same age as I. He is the son of one of our serfs; a good industrious family, and well respected by my father.

Sevaric works with the raw wool and applies himself with dedication and principle. He is fair of hair—his family being from the north. He is well formed and strong—much stronger than I. I have seen him often staring at me with a longing that I knew signaled a desire for more accomplishment than his restricted life has offered him thus far. He has a sparkle in his eye that shows intelligence and a drive to excel.

One morning I stood watching him, unseen, as he manipulated the sacks of raw wool, preparing them for carding. He easily hoisted the sacks onto his strong shoulders and moved them adroitly into the next room. Upon his return he spotted me and stopped, looking at me with his sharp hazel eyes. He smiled at me, and then moved on to the next sack to be moved.

I called out to him, "Sevaric."

"Sir?" He stopped with a load on his shoulders.

"Come to the counting chamber when you have disposed of that," I commanded, with perhaps too strong a demand.

"Sir," he answered briskly, and disappeared into the carding room.

I returned to my chamber and awaited his appearance. Duly he arrived and entered, holding his grubby hat in his hands, wringing it with some anxiety. He stood quietly in front of me waiting for me to speak first, unsure as to the nature of my summons.

"You may sit if you like," I stated, indicating a chair across from my writing table.

He smiled with some relief and pulled up the chair so he was close by me. I could smell the strong odor of raw wool and sweat emanating from his coarse shirt. He looked at me with great focus and intensity. I studied him for a moment. I felt very strongly that I had been correct in my assessment of his abilities.

"Sevaric, I have been watching your work here and have been very pleased with what I have seen."

He regarded me with a slight smile and a nod and waited, not responding otherwise.

"Let me ask you a question. Have you had any schooling?"

"Yes, sir. My mother is from a good family up north and she has had a fair amount of learning, and taught me both reading and writing. Also some music."

'Music?"

"I can read music, and I can play the cittern."

I nodded, wondering why I had not noticed this man before now. "I am impressed. Then why are you working here in this laborious position?"

"Sir, it is what my family does. Where else could I go? I am not a gentleman like yourself."

"Can you copy this out for me?" I handed him a page of accounts.

He studied it a moment and answered. "Sir, this is mostly numbers. Are you sure this is what you want me to copy? I can read and copy full pages of text as well."

"Yes, for now, just do that for me."

He proceeded to copy the page, seated at the edge of my table across from me; handing it to me, completed in a fine hand, when he was finished.

"Now, read this." I handed him, this time, a book on loan from the Fathers.

He took it and read flawlessly. He looked up at me when he had finished the first page. "More?" he asked.

"Not necessary." He handed the book back to me. "Now, a question for you." I hesitated a moment, enjoying creating a little suspense for Sevaric as he waited for my proposal. "I am very impressed with your accomplishments. And you seem to be a very engaging and bright young man. I very much need some assistance with my work both in this counting room and on the floor, and I would like you to assist me."

Sevaric smiled but did not give into any overt emotion. "Will there be a pay increase?" he finally asked.

I held my official face, but a slight twinkle in my eyes gave me away. "Yes, that is very likely."

"And, Sir, do you think it possible I might be able to borrow some books from you on occasion? I very much hunger to read more, but books are generally not available to me."

This was a moment of great happiness for me. I had found not only a capable assistant, but I believed I had found a new friend as well.

Twentieth of March 1347

Again it is late at night. And though I fear I may suffer from lack of sleep tomorrow, I am once again drawn to continue my narration. Tonight it is almost warm, and I have my casement open to the night breeze.

I have not heard my wolf tonight. Perhaps he has found some peace. I hope it is not because he has encountered a farmer's trap and is no longer with us. I should miss his friendship greatly, as I do believe he knows of me as I know of him.

I shall now continue my story.

The taking on of Sevaric as my assistant proved to be a wise decision. He learned quickly and became an adept companion both at the warehouse and on the outside as well, as he was an expert hunter and would accompany me on my painful expeditions to find game for both his table and mine. Not that I ever grew to enjoy this sport, but I did look forward to our adventures together, where we would talk of music and books, and the differences in our lives, while we scouted for game in the hills of our estate. Though, because I was his master, I always had to take the lead in our conversations—much to my sadness, as I always enjoyed hearing his unbridled and spontaneous thoughts when they would break through with his unguarded enthusiasm.

I am reminded of one occasion in particular. We had just come up empty-handed after a brace of quail escaped our capture, and our traps were coming up empty. The day was hot, as it was now mid-June. We sought the comfort of shade and the cooling influence of a small natural pond secluded deep in the woods.

I lay down on the bank by the water. A willow hung overhead and the branches barely swayed because of the stifling heat and the stillness of the air. Sevaric lay down beside me. While I was on my back, staring up at the interior of the willow, he lay on his side, his head supported by his arm, and he looked at me deeply and with a strange expression. A leaf fluttered down from the tree above and landed on my forehead. I was too lazy to even turn my head to dislodge it. Sevaric reached over with his free hand and gently brushed it away. I turned to look at him. Our eyes met and he smiled very slightly.

"How about a swim?" he asked, as he rose and began to undress.

I, being extremely shy about my slight build, and not an accomplished swimmer, declined, but sat up and watched as he undressed. His body was strong and firm, excellently well proportioned, and he gleefully ran towards the water and plunged in. His head emerging from the depths, he shook it like a wet Spaniel, his longish blond hair swirling off a glistening spray. He laughed and played, crossing the pond several times with a strong swimmers stroke. He called out to me.

"You should really come in. It is very cooling in this heat. Just a little way if you are afraid," he taunted, almost daring me.

I stood up and walked to the edge of the pond and crouched down and put my hand in the water. Even that slight contact was refreshing. The grasses at the edge bent down into the water, inviting me to just slip in. However, there was something else going on with me that prevented me from moving forward. While I had greatly appreciated Sevaric's company for some time now, I also was beginning to recognize a new feeling that was unfamiliar and a bit disturbing. I could not take my eyes off his body gliding through the water like a beguiling serpent. I felt a stirring in my – I am reluctant to utter the word, but shall use the common word I have heard on occasion from the workers in the warehouse – cock.

I did not understand this phenomenon, as I believe this is a response that is reserved for one's wife. I have little knowledge of these things, as I have had very little education about such matters. However, my father has promised me a talk before my marriage with Celestria. Not that I have not relieved myself many times, alone in my bed in the mornings when I would awake with my member stiff and aching for release. I understood this. But this was happening to me now as I watched Sevaric, so graceful, strong and gleaming in the water. This could not be right. Though I have had some such inklings before when I would come upon a groom nearly naked in the barn on a hot day tending to our horses. But these stirrings I dismissed as flushes caused by the heat and lack of appropriate exercise. But this today was something else. This had been building in me throughout the day. Besides the great pleasure I derived from Sevaric's company, I was aware that I wanted to be physically near him as well. I would position myself so that our shoulders would touch, or I would brush his hand as we examined a trap together. I remembered the look in his eyes, just now, as we relaxed beneath the tree, and I have no idea what that look signified.

Just then Sevaric swam over to me at the edge of the pond. He put his hands on the bank, on either side of where I was still crouching. I could not stand up because of my state of arousal, which would surely show. He did not speak, but just looked up at me, again with that mischievous smile—his eyes burning into my depths, throwing me into further confusion. I could not speak, either. He playfully splashed some water at me and laughed, leaning back and pushing off from the shore with the force of his strong legs. I could see that he too had the same problem as I.

I quickly stood and turned away so he could not see my condition. I called out to him, "I think we'd better go now. We need to find some game before we return, or both our families will be displeased."

He forcefully swam to the shore and pulled himself out of the water, still in an aroused condition, but he did not seem to mind, or be embarrassed by it in any way. He

quickly dried himself with his shirt, dressed and
presented himself to me ready to continue the hunt.

Second of April 1347

It has been difficult for me come back to this
correspondence, as what I am now to recite pains me, and
I have a great deal of guilt about what is to follow.

I am afraid that as a result of my discoveries about
myself that day at the pond, I have behaved badly.
Instead of finding some way to punish my own wayward
flesh I turned my confusion and inner torment into a
desire to punish Sevaric. I became very cold to him at the
warehouse. I refused his entreaties to accompany me
hunting—and was especially adamant about avoiding
swims—and I harshly refused to lend him any of my
books. He took it very badly. While he would never utter
a word of protest, or reproach me in any way, I could see
the pain and bewilderment in his eyes—those beautiful
hazel eyes.

I foolishly urged my father to hasten the wedding,
and he was greatly pleased with that, and arranged an
engagement banquet for the next month. It was to be a
grand affair in the fullness of summer. The house was in
constant activity as my father was hosting many of the
finest families in the district. The kitchen was bursting
with game, slaughtered domestic animals, great cakes,
pies both sweet and savory, and mounds of fruits and
vegetables fresh from our orchards and gardens. My
sisters were recruited to fashion masses of garlands for
both interior and exterior decoration. It took two days for
the servants to prepare the dining hall. Again an
abundance of flowers graced the tables, and there was a

bevy of servants carefully measuring each place setting and amassing an army of candles.

My father engaged the very best tailor of the district to fashion new attire for the entire family; all of us fitted out most elegantly, befitting our wealth and station.

I, by this time, was embroiled in many conflicting emotions. I was disgusted by what I considered to be the excesses of this pending event. I realized that I had been rash in persuading my father to push ahead with the wedding, and was dreading having to spend so much time and attention on Celestria, who would be increasingly in my company after the engagement. It was beginning to dawn on me that I would be marrying her in October, and I would be forever linked to her, and cut off from so many of my solitary freedoms and joys.

And my self-isolation from Sevaric was a new and growing pain. With all the constant activity and duties surrounding the impending banquet I had barely attended to my work at the warehouse, which accorded, however, with my father's wishes. It wasn't until the day of the event itself that I was to learn that Sevaric was to personally serve Celestria and me at the banquet supper. My father had recognized the same qualities in Sevaric that I had, and persuaded him to serve us, thinking it would be a compliment to me, as I had discovered and promoted him. But for me it was both a great pain and a great joy. I was racked with guilt over my treatment of him, and found, that instead of my feelings abating, they were enflamed by our separation. I would toss in my bed at night, haunted by the image of him emerging from the pond—golden, wet, erect.

The day before the banquet, tormented and unsettled, I took my horse and rode off by myself into the woods without telling anyone where I was going. I returned to our pond, and throwing myself on the bank where we had lain, wept—letting out a cry that I prayed would be heard by no one. I cried myself into a slumber and awoke just before dusk, knowing I would be missed at the house and would incur my father's wrath when I returned.

As I awoke, I sensed a presence across the pond. I had slept deeply in my grief and had a difficult time focusing in the dusk. I lifted myself into a seated position and stared across the water. There on the far bank was a wolf. He stared at me for a long time, then raised his head and let out a howl, and finally turned and disappeared into the darkness of the surrounding woods. I would grow to know that cry. I would hear it many nights in the solitude of my chamber. His cry would later become my cry.

Seventh of April 1347

Again I have been absent from my recitation for a week now. The pain of looking at these shortcomings of mine has prevented me from returning until now. But I feel an urgency to complete this, as events outside of my control may soon interrupt this narrative in ways I cannot now comprehend.

I must now, with some anguish, relate the events of the day of the banquet. The morning broke with a splendid sky. A dawn of rose and pale yellow bespoke of happy nuptials – for all but me. I had been soundly scolded for my absence the afternoon and early evening before the banquet. My father's fury was only mitigated by his pleasure in the morrow's events. He quickly dismissed his anger and moved quickly to engage me in a hearty discussion of the joys of matrimony, including the "talk" he had promised me concerning my husbandly duties. I was mortified with embarrassment, and so, as it turned out, was he. The discussion ended up being mercifully brief.

It had been a long time since the village and district had witnessed such a stunning event as our banquet. Carriages, carts and horses drew up to our entrance. Our grooms were frantic tending to the many arrivals. It could not have been a more perfect day, as a storm had moved through during the previous night, and the morning was clear and cooler than usual, preventing excessive discomfort in our packed dining hall.

I will not dwell on the banquet itself, except to say it was lavish and was all that my father had hoped for. My bride to be was at my side and we exchanged minimal conversation as her mother was on my other side and constantly plied me with a running commentary on the event, and endless questions about our business and financial success. However, I paid her scant attention as my focus was elsewhere.

Sevaric stood obediently behind me. He was dressed in the household livery. While he was attentive to Celestria, he was lavish in his attention to me. He refilled my goblet practically after each sip of wine I took. It did not go unnoticed by me that each time he leaned forward he would brush my shoulder, or his hand would lightly touch my neck as he whisked away a fly. Again, I was overcome by the same sensations that had plagued me at the pond the day of his swim. Luckily I was wearing a jacket that covered the most prominent manifestation of my discomfort. But I could not help but notice that Sevaric suffered the same indignation as me, though he covered it well from all but me to see. A moment came when our eyes met for a brief second. He could not suppress his shy but devastating smile. I became both enflamed and chilled at the same moment. My hand began to shake as I raised the goblet to drink in an attempt to quell my flushes and violent feelings. Celestria seemed to notice my agitation and turned to me.

"Are you well, my beloved?" she asked, placing her delicate hand on my arm.

I looked down at her hand then up into her eyes, which I am sure would enflame many another manly breast. I nodded, for I could not speak just then.

"It may be the heat. I find this hall to be extremely cloistering with this amount of guests. Will you please excuse me a moment?" I finally asked. She nodded, and as I arose her mother looked at me with a peculiar expression as I passed behind her.

Sevaric reached out to me as I escaped and asked, "Do you need my assistance sir?"

I stopped and looked at him. "Not just yet." And I fled out of the hall, my father looking after me with some concern.

I rushed to my chambers and splashed water on my face and the back of my neck and then sat on the edge of my bed and collected my thoughts and my breath, as I had been breathing hard short breaths as I escaped the hall.

Finally, composing myself, and shedding some of the heavy outer garments that the formal occasion required, I returned to the banquet hall.

I will not relate the torture of the endless lines of well-wishers I had to endure, nor the agony of the relentless barrage of questioning from the pending in-laws. Just let it be noted that finally the ghastly event ended, and I escaped to my rooms to surrender the formal garments that restricted and enchained me.

I was desperate to escape outside and embrace the cool evening that had finally settled in; relieving me, as a gentle breeze picked up, and I began to, once again, feel a moment of tranquility and peace.

I wandered away from the house, past the barns, with the grooms still active as they put to rest the horses, still skittish from the unusual quartering of the guest's strange mounts in their midst.

I wandered past the house gardens and orchards and into a field of corn, now grown up to the height of my waist. From there I found a sloping bank at the edge of the field covered in an array of wild flowers. I sat down and watched as the moon rose over the forest across the field. I was very near the edge of tears, once again, as I felt the depth of my sorrow, brought on solely by my own foolish actions. I lay back against the bank, closed my eyes and contemplated rash actions I might take that would only further enflame my precarious condition. I imagined flight to a foreign realm, sequestration with a sympathetic order of religious devotees, and even, I am ashamed to relate, self-annihilation.

Then, with but the faintest brush of a gentle kiss I heard whispered in my ear, "Do you need my assistance now, sir?"

I opened my eyes to see Sevaric stretched out beside me. I had not heard, nor sensed, his approach and his reclining down beside me. That is how deeply I was entranced by my own sorrow. I did not react with either shock or fear. I simply stared into his eyes, now clearly visible by the fullness of the moon. His kiss had not only awoken me, but also transformed me. I had crossed a threshold and was no longer a slave to indecision or guilt. I reached over and put my hand softly on his cheek.

"Can you forgive me?" I asked from a heart aching with longing and desire.

He barely stirred. "But there has been no hurt. There is nothing to forgive." He buried his head between my shoulder and my neck and ever so lightly gave me another kiss. I turned towards him and took his head in my hands and brought him to me, and for the first time in my life I knew who I was.

Eighth of May 1347

Again, too long an absence from this discourse. I have read over the preceding lines many times and am astonished at what I have written. Why am I committing this to a hard reality that could be discovered and cause my ruination? I only know I must.

I have been married now since September last. The reason for the earlier date will be explained further along.

My wife is still not pregnant, and unlikely to become so. I have refused to perform my marital duties, and my poor desperate wife wildly accuses herself in my failing. How can I begin to console her, for she is such a sweet, innocent and uncomplicated creature?

I write this in part for her. It is what I would tell her if I could. By writing this I feel that I am somehow easing her soul, even if she will never know the truth of this story from me in her present life.

I pass now from that night in the field. For me it was the true beginning of my life. My forever hidden life, I believed at that time. Suffice it to say, I discovered that evening what my whole being had been trying to get me to acknowledge for a long time. That day of betrothal to Celestria became, in fact, my night of marriage to Sevaric.

From that time forward we were nearly inseparable. We had to continue our façade at the warehouse. He was my assistant and I was his master, but we slipped, without too much discomfort, into our new relationship, masked by the conventions of our stations and work duties. He never questioned our need to conceal our affections.

Though we had consummated our relationship that night in the field, we have never really spent an entire night together in a bed and awoken together the next morning in each other's arms as we both so much longed to do. We have had to be satisfied, instead, with our tenuous encounters in the fields or woods, far from prying eyes. Happy though these moments were, we both still longed for our own privacy and a deeper, more prolonged and intimate connection.

But an opportunity would soon present itself, which we could not then anticipate with greater joy. It was time for me to travel once again to Strasbourg with our latest shipment of merchandise, with a final destination down river on the barges. And I, of course, would need my assistant.

Our journey would comprise a full day's journey to Strasbourg, an additional day of negotiation and unloading the shipment, and a third day's return home. That meant two nights together at the inn. It is not uncommon for two men to share a room while traveling, even sharing the same bed, as lodging is scarce and beds even scarcer. You cannot imagine how eagerly we looked forward to that trip.

But as our journey was still several weeks away, we wanted to find agreeable activities to pass the remaining time. Sevaric's enthusiasms were almost like those of a child, and he insisted that I be presented to his family, even though I could not reciprocate by inviting him to meet mine.

"Please," he pleaded one evening, as we left the warehouse and walked together towards our homes.

"But how would it look?" I asked in answer to his invitation.

"But you are my master," he answered. "We can make up some reason for you to visit. It would not be untoward for you to call at your serf's house. We can say you have come for an inspection of the property – for tax purposes, let's say. Then it would be only hospitable to offer you some refreshment. You could stay and enter into conversation and before long I could bring out the instruments and my mother and I could perform for you. Before you knew it, we would have a whole evening together. What do you say?"

I nodded my head in thought. How I longed for us to be open together. And how greatly I wished to hold him in front of his family and kiss the back of his neck as I had seen my father do with my mother. "Yes, I think that might be possible," I finally answered. We then walked together in silence, and he dared to take my hand in the gathering dusk.

"Are there others like us?" I asked, unafraid to so show my ignorance about such matters.

"There are."

"How do you know? Have you been with a man before me?"

He looked at me, not quite sure how he should answer me, for fear he might upset me.

"I don't mind if you have," I finally said to ease his confusion.

"I have," he answered. "But not many. There are places in the village where men can meet. But I have been with no one else since we have been together. Nor do I wish to."

"Where in the village?" I wanted to know as much as I could about who we were.

"Why do you want to know? Want to sample other wares?" he teased and poked me in the arm.

"Just curious. I know so little."

"Well, there is a place at the edge of the market, not far from the mill. And there is a place under the main bridge out of town, but only at night."

"And you have been to these places?"

He nodded. "But not often."

"Are there many of us?"

"More than you might imagine."

He leaned over and gave me a quick kiss on the cheek, as we were now at the point in the road where we had to part for our several ways home. He ran off with a quick look back at me and waved, as I stood and watched him till he had completely disappeared.

How greatly we both anticipated our journey to Strasbourg. We would recite the details of the trip together over and over again until the day finally arrived.

Sevaric was early to the warehouse that glorious day. It was now mid August and it would be hot. We wanted to get an early start, to get as much travel time in as possible while it was still cool in the morning.

When I arrived he had already bridled the oxen, as the carts had been loaded and prepared for travel the day before. I made a quick inspection of the merchandise, gave final instructions to the supervisor at the warehouse, and we set out—a very respectable looking merchant and his assistant.

We traveled together most of the morning in silence. We each had to attend to the driving of a cart and so were separated and preoccupied with that task. However, we would shout out to each other on occasion, pointing out a feature in the landscape or throwing the water flask between us from cart to cart.

Just before noon we pulled off the road. Since I had made this trip many times before I knew of this secluded resting place. A quiet field bordered a sparking stream, rushing briskly towards the Rhine. We uncoupled the oxen and let them drink and graze. I pulled out the basket my mother had prepared for the trip. A gaggle of geese honked across the stream and seemed to protest our intrusion upon their acknowledged terrain. We sought comfort under a tree near the brook, secluded from inspection from the road, and spread out a hearty mid-day meal before us. Both of us were hungry and quickly satisfied ourselves with my mother's delicious contribution to our journey.

We lay back against the trunk of a large Sycamore and closed our eyes briefly, enjoying the peace and the sound of the brook, coolly passing beside us. Sevaric reached over and took my hand. I opened my eyes and turned towards him. His eyes were still closed, but he had a look of such sweet contentment that I could not bring myself to disturb this tranquil moment. Slowly he opened his eyes and turned towards me and we leaned towards each other and kissed. Little did I know what that kiss would eventually cost us.

I knew that we would have to arrive at the shipping yards in Strasbourg before they were closed and secured for the night. We needed to store our carts and merchandise in the yard for protection. So after our refreshment, we corralled the oxen, bridled them, and progressed on our way.

The rest of the afternoon was uneventful, but we were spurred on by our desire to reach the city and finally be alone together. We actually arrived a little early, disposed of the carts, secured the oxen for the night, and repaired as quickly as possible to the inn.

By my foresight I had written to the inn in advance and reserved the very best room for our stay. We decided that during our first evening we would have our dinner in the room and spend the remainder of the evening in each other's arms.

There are some things that I cannot put down in this discourse, even if they will never be read by anyone but me. Some events so private and glorious, that I cannot find the words to express them, even to myself.

Suffice it to say, that to us, our union was sacred. I am very well aware that this statement is blasphemy in the eyes of the world I live in now. And I am aware that we are threatened with forever damnation in the eyes of that world. By that world's standards, in the life hereafter, my mind and my soul may be forever in torment; but my body knows differently. Somewhere there is a realm where our love is real, recognized and honored. I may never find that place, but I know it exists. I will forever celebrate our union, and no man, woman, churchman, lieutenant, officer or king on high can negate our love. Do what they may; my soul and very being shall ever resist their ignorant tyranny.

Too soon came the end of our business in Strasbourg, and it was time to return home. Sevaric was in the shipping yard bridling the oxen. We had bought provisions to transport home in the empty carts. I slipped away, unseen, for just a moment. There was a silversmith's stall just around the corner. I made a quick purchase and returned before Sevaric even noticed I was gone.

We proceeded on our journey home, and stopped again at the field and brook for our lunch, purchased from the inn. As we sat at the base of the Sycamore, having just finished eating, I reached over and took Sevaric's hand. He looked up at me.

I reached into my pocket and took out the two silver rings I had bought from the smith. I didn't say a word but slipped one ring on his finger and then one on mine. He just leaned forward and took me in his arms tears streaming down his face.

"Oh, Warin..." was all he could say.

We separated and looked at each other as we held hands, still seated on the ground.

"I wanted us to wear them now. But when we get back home, they must not be seen." I pulled out two chains. "We must wear them like this." I took off my ring and put it on the chain, then the chain around my neck, and tucked it inside my shirt. "Close to my heart."

He did the same. Then he held his hand over the ring inside his shirt.

"Forever," he said, and we nodded to each other.

Twelfth of May 1347

News and rumors have been rampant in the county the past few days. It seems that a barge pulled into port in Strasbourg recently, and it is reported that many of the crew were dead or dying from the plague. The ship was immediately quarantined, but that has not quelled the panic, nor stopped the locals from arming themselves to ward off strangers coming into the area. I am afraid we shall now be entering into a time of even more mistrust and violence.

I feel that I must act quickly to complete this narration as I do not know if we will have to retire to another part of the country, or even if my own health will be endangered in any way.

To continue the story: My beloved Sevaric and I returned home from our journey to Strasbourg. It had been a very successful venture financially, as we have been promised a handsome price for our goods when they reach their final destination. My father did seem pleased with the results; but surprisingly, he responded with much less enthusiasm than I had anticipated. But for Sevaric and me the significance of the journey was not in the success of the business, but in the happiness we shared together at the inn.

It was very difficult for Sevaric and me the first few days after our return. We had become accustomed, in just a short while, to openly express our affection for each other, and to experience our equality together. So it came as a great shock to be back in the warehouse as master and serf. We were developing, however, a new language of looks and gestures that was known only to us, and provided us with some comfort when we were in public together.

Never once were we able to be alone together through an entire night as we had been in Strasbourg, but we were still able to meet secretly, away from our homes or the warehouse. But it would not be too long before autumn and winter would arrive, and we would have to seek more accommodating places to meet than the open countryside.

Then one morning we had an unexpected opportunity to be together again in an intimate way. It was a Sunday and my entire family was off at church. I remained behind, as we were expecting a new horse from Paris, and I was elected to greet the handlers when they arrived.

I was out in the barn overseeing the preparation of a stall for the new stallion, when I spied Sevaric walking through the open field near the spot where we had first united. I called out to him. He saw me and came running over, arriving flushed and breathless. I finished my inspection of the horse accommodations and invited him to follow me, making sure that I was very proper in my relations with him in front of the grooms.

We went into the kitchen, but all of the servants, too, were at church. Away from prying eyes I took him in my arms, and then said, "Come." I lead him up the back stairs to my residential wing and we secluded ourselves behind my closed and locked door. I knew we only had a brief time together, as I could see where the sun touched my writing table and could calculate how far it would travel before my family would return from church.

I flung Sevaric onto my bed and we satisfied ourselves in an almost violent manner, such was our pent up passion. Lying together after, I gazed into his eyes and put my hand up to his cheek.

"You have not shaved today," I commented, kissing his cheek and feeling the stubble.

"Is it too rough for you?"

I shook my head. "It makes you seem more comely."

"Then I shall never shave again."

I laughed. "No, I would not like you with a full beard either. You would seem too much like my father, and that would put me off completely," I teased.

He looked at me again without speaking for quite some time and then at last spoke. "Warin, you will be marrying soon." I could see the sadness in his eyes. "What will happen to us then?"

"There will be nothing different for us. For my father the marriage is only about the property he wants to acquire. For me, my marriage has already occurred – that night in the field, and again in Strasbourg.

"But you will have duties to perform as a married man."

I reflected upon his words for a moment. "Yes, so I have been told. But I honestly do not know if I am capable of that. And what about you? Won't your parents expect you to marry soon?"

"I will not marry another, I am already married."

"But your family, won't they insist?"

"My mother knows about us, and will not insist."

I was shocked. "You told her?"

He laughed. "No, she told me."

"What?"

"She is a very perceptive woman. It did not take her long to understand us. Especially after that night you visited us and we played music."

"And she is not angry? Did she tell your father?"

"No to both of your questions."

Just then I heard the sound of horses and a carriage pulling up in front of the house. I jumped out of bed, rushed to the window, and saw my family alighting from our carriage; and at the same time the drovers arrived with our new stallion.

"Dress!" I shouted. "I have not watched the hour closely enough." I rushed to him and took him in my arms as he was trying to put on his pants. He struggled and laughed. But I held tightly, as though it would be our last time together, for I did not know when we would be able to share this bed again.

I must stop here now. I am overcome with the thoughts of what is to come. I need to prepare myself to continue later.

Fifteenth of May 1347

Despite my great heartache, I must complete this narrative.

Not long after that Sunday when Sevaric and I had shared my bed, there came a morning when breakfast was very tense and unusually strange. My father was restless and would not look me in the eye. I suspected that he and my mother had quarreled, and dismissed it as a family matter that did not concern me.

I appeared at the warehouse, prepared to work, expecting to find Sevaric, who was usually there before me. I enquired of the other workers if they had seen him; I thought perhaps he had gone on an errand. But he had not been seen at all that day.

I went to the counting room and began my work. I became engrossed in some accounts and was slow to react when the door opened. I looked up with a great smile, expecting to see Sevaric, but instead beheld my father. He had a very grim expression, and I began to suspect that his behavior that morning at breakfast might have concerned me without my knowing it.

"Good morning, again, Father," I tried to greet him with some welcome in my voice. "We have not seen you here for some time. Is there a problem?" I began to suspect that he was going to chastise me for some improper accounts, or that there might be a problem with the up-coming shearing.

"You are to come with me now." Was all he said, but it was very clear that there was some great trouble at hand.

I arose from my table and accompanied him, not into the warehouse as I expected, but out to the street and towards the town square. He grabbed my arm with great force, hurting me, and led me forward without a single word.

"Father, what is going on? Please explain to me what the trouble is." I was beginning to become deeply frightened.

"I saw you—during your trip to Strasbourg. You and that *boy*—kissing in a field. Such indecency! I have been troubled about you for some time. Now I know why."

"You? How?"

"The day of your departure for Strasbourg, I needed to present you with some letters that I wanted delivered. You were already gone when I arrived at the warehouse. I followed after, and came upon the both of you while you were stopped in that field."

"Then why didn't you present yourself to us?"

"I was not alone. Magistrate Baldoc had accompanied me. We were so shocked I did not know how to proceed. We returned home."

"Oh God." I looked around me, hoping to see Sevaric. "Where is he? What will happen?"

"Your family name has saved you lad, but there must be consequences."

"Where are we going? Where is Sevaric? Has something happened to him?"

"You best be concerned only for yourself, just now. It has taken a great effort on my part to keep you out of this."

"Father..."

By now we had reached the town square. There was quite a large crowd pushing towards the center and it was growing by the minute. My father pulled me into a doorway and up a flight of stairs at the town hall. We emerged into an empty chamber. He pulled me over to a small balcony and we stood looking down on the square below. In the center of the square was a scaffolding, a central pillar, and surrounding it a large construction of faggots for a fire. I knew immediately what it was and turned to flee, desperate to find Sevaric and save him. My father, being a much stronger man than I, grabbed me and held me firmly, forcing me to take in the scene as it unfolded below.

My father gave a nod to someone I could not see, and immediately Sevaric appeared in the company of several officers. His mother rushed forward and clung to him, screaming and crying. She was pulled violently away, and Sevaric was led directly to the scaffolding and tied securely to the central pillar. His arms were not restricted, so that he would be allowed to pray. He was close enough so that I could clearly see his face. He was not in fear. He scanned the crowd, saw me, and smiled his secret smile. I could not cry out to him as my father had his hand over my mouth so I would not betray myself.

The crowd started to become restless and agitated. They pushed in closer to the center. A magistrate read out a proclamation accusing Sevaric of sodomy and unnatural acts against God, and the crowd responded with cries of "Light the faggots! Light the faggots! Burn!"

The magistrate raised his hand and the crowd quieted momentarily. He gestured towards two men standing by the side with lighted torches. They came forward and, touching the fire to the base of the prepared woodpile, the flames shot quickly upwards. The crowd became frantic, chanting their cries of "burn" and dancing wildly around the pyre as though it was a special holiday.

Sevaric remained calm. He spoke not a word, but having found me, his gaze never left me. He reached up with his free hand and pulled out the ring on the chain around his neck. He held it out towards me until the flames engulfed him and his head fell forward, like when I had seen him nod off, just before he fell asleep at my side. I closed my eyes, still securely in my father's arms, but no tears would come. For me there was only the smell of his burning flesh.

Twentieth of May 1347

Our worst fears are being realized. I have heard reports that a case of the plague has been discovered in the village. I have been conferring with my family about what course of action we must all take, but there have been no firm plans yet formed. I feel even more urgency now to complete my tale.

After Sevaric's death I refused to set foot ever again in the warehouse. I confined myself to my chambers for weeks. I refused to take meals with the family, and I would not speak with my father. Twice I tried escaping the county, hoping to head for Paris, but each time my father and his men caught up with me and forced me home, driving me deeper into my seclusion.

My father decided he needed to move the wedding up to September, incorrectly believing that the love of a true woman would be my cure. Never was there a more recalcitrant groom. I have to admit that I was most cruel to my poor bride. She does not deserve me, and I pray that one day she might find herself a true lover. For my part, I shall never seek, nor do I expect to find, the quality of love that I so richly experienced with Sevaric. I have been told that in time wounds heal, pain fades, and yes, even love will diminish. I have, as of yet, not found that to be true.

It has been just over half a year now since I lost all that I was, or ever hoped to be. I exist—yes just exist. Each day I awake, move through my duties of the day and retire once again—alone in my own bed. I have not returned to the pond, nor ever expect to. I abide with that sweet woman whom I honor as my wife, but do not love.

And our childlessness galls my father; I feel that it is just retribution for his hateful actions towards me.

I am now up to date with my story. I do not know if this is the end of my narration or not. I know there is no end to my sorrow. These few lines have given me comfort as I wander back in my mind to the time in my life when I was truly alive. I do not see how I can endure the remainder of my time here on earth, and long solely to be reunited with my Sevaric in our special place. Only time, and God's Will, can reveal when that will be.

I will put these pages aside for now, and later, if there is anything of importance to report I shall return. If not, then I turn this poor narrative over to my destiny and remain....

Warin of the House of Thann

Twenty-second of August 1347

I awoke this morning with a pain so deep that I can hardly breathe. It is one year ago today that Sevaric was taken from me. But I must not dwell on that now. There is no time to waste. The plague has ravaged our area. With great sorrow I must report the death of my two sisters, my mother and my wife. My father is not well, and will probably not survive.

While I am still well, I feel that I must flee this area. I have requested, and been invited, to reside with the brothers at the Ascenseur Monastery. It is my understanding that all there are still well, and they have carefully sealed themselves off from the surrounding pestilence. They are self-sufficient and require no outside assistance to continue in their good health. I am very grateful that they will allow me to join them.

It is time now for me to depart. I shall report more later if there are any further developments of consequence.

Ninth of September 1347

How much anguish can a single person endure? All around me is falling into ruin. My father did, indeed, perish. The infection has entered the Monastery and many of the Brothers have fallen victim to the plague. For some reason, I have been spared. I do all that I can each day to tend to those who are ill, but there is no treatment, and I fall into bed each night exhausted from my duties. And it is a great effort now to write even these few brief words. I can write no more this evening.

Third of October 1347

There is little time left now. I, too, have become a victim of this disease. I am covered in blisters and can barely drink even a small amount of water, though I have a high fever, and at times find myself falling into delirium.

I feel my life has prepared me well for my end, and I look forward with such great joy to my final release. Oh, my beloved, Sevaric, I shall soon be with you.

(The following is written in a hand other than that of the author of this manuscript)

Tenth of October 1347

Sevaric, I am with you now.

Sierra Dunn

With a partner of eight years and a cat muse by her side, Sierra Dunn pens insights into her voyage of self-discovery, highlighting for all the strength of who we already are. Her new album, "Release" (she's a musician and song-writer, as well) is available on iTunes. Sierra creates lyrics from the heart, but they do some winding through hell before making it out alive. Her words sprout from a reservoir of deep earth, then flourish skyward in a heat of growth as the reader/listener becomes entwined and enlightened to the solid realization that *this isn't just another story... it's My Story... no, no, wait... it's Everyone's story*. A former Portlander now living in Philly, Sierra celebrates her role in the GLBTQ creative community.

Recovery

This is what I have
Got to find a way to Love it.

I Hold myself bleeding
I Hold myself grieving
I wipe away my tears
The bigger part of me knows All is Well
My body comes and goes
I turn Translucent when I Know I am That, Everything

Thankful for my healthy body
My Abilities
So long spent feeling ugly
Wasted time in this body
Could've been loving myself

Always done the best I could.
Always given myself opportunities to surprise myself

Just came slowly,
Or maybe quicker than some?
Still coming
Layers drop and the resistance burns and kicks and
screams for mercy.
Burns away

What is left
Is Self Trust
Love
A Grander Awareness
Peace
Rest
And the Ability to Get On with it.

I am in the Recovery
From Decades of Self Abuse
My Grander self, I've learned soul neglect
Retrace back my steps
To Home.

The self-hate
The Projections I cast
The Attraction to what I most Fear
The manifesting of the gruesome names I most dread to hear

I am Larger than that
I am Bigger that that
This is where I make my Home
I am okay with how it goes
I am in command of my own self love
Self nurturance
And I will be until the end
I have the reins

I will always be with me
There for me
To hold me when I need comfort
To assure me I am bigger, to show me
To assure me I am safe, made up of the universe, the Bigness
Outstretched
To assure me I am love
To thank every step
Along the path
To caress the tired cheek
Ready to give up
Ready to let go
Ready to release everything
And live

Contributors Page

Like what you've read? Help support our contributing authors by checking out their books or albums. Also in print or ebook by:

David Matthew Barnes
   Accidents Never Happen
   Ambrosia
   The Jetsetters
   Mesmerized
   Swimming to Chicago
   Wonderland

Georgia Beers
   96 Hours
   Too Close to Touch
   Mine
   The Neighbor's Wife
   Turning the Page
   Finding Home
   Starting From Scratch
   Fresh Tracks

Brad Craddock
   Alice's Misadventures Underground
   The Curse of the Dark Woods

Sierra Dunn
   Release (album)

Tony Leuzzi
   Radiant Losses
   Fake Book
   Passwords Primeval
   40, 000 Crows

Jon McDonald
Divas Never Flinch
Bloodlines – the Quest
The Seed
Snapshots

Christine Noble
Ego Codex
Drawing Lines

Shauna Marie O'Toole
You Can't Shave in a Minimart Bathroom
My Transition Checklist
Recycled

Damian Serbu
The Vampire's Angel series:
The Vampire's Angel
The Vampire's Quest
The Vampire's Witch (2013)
Secrets in the Attic
Dark Sorcerer Threatening

Thomas Warfield
Celebrate the Moment (album)

Cover Photography

Eleanor Leonne Bennett

Eleanor Leonne Bennett is a 16 year old internationally award winning photographer and artist who has won first places with National Geographic, The World Photography Organization, Nature's Best Photography, Papworth Trust, Mencap, The Woodland trust and Postal Heritage. Her photography has been published in the Telegraph, The Guardian, BBC News Website and on the cover of books and magazines in the United States and Canada. Her art is globally exhibited.

Editors

Gregory Gerard

Gregory Gerard's work has been published by Tiny Lights, The Stone Table Review, and World Voice. He teaches writing part-time at Writers & Books, Rochester's contemporary literary center, and has been a guest instructor at the University of Rochester's Scholars Creative Writing Program. Gerard's memoir, *In Jupiter's Shadow*, (2009, Infinity Publishing) chronicles a religious boy's struggle with forbidden attraction. It explores how we all receive messages about what we "should be" in life and how we sometimes work to hide truth from the most important person in our lives: ourselves.

Lou Cinelli

Lou spent almost four decades in CA, graduating USC, then teaching Speech/Theatre. He returned to the Rochester area seven years ago and is a newly minted docent at the Memorial Art Gallery, reader to the Blind at WXXI, swimmer/kayaker at Sodus Point, and aging climber of mountains—anywhere. Lou's also wild about Harry, and Tom, and Dick—who don't know he exists, so he travels often and sees lots of movies along the way.

KaeLyn E.L. Rich

KaeLyn Rich is a (femme)nist ladypoet and Queer-Vegan-Korean-Immigrant-Ms. America-Pageant winner. She formerly penned "The Vagina Dialogues," a queer women's health column in *The Empty Closet* and has blogged on Feminists and Sex, Justice, Change. Her poetry was featured at the 2004 National Women's Studies Association. KaeLyn holds degrees in Creative Writing and Women's Studies from SUNY College at Oswego. These days, KaeLyn is a full-time activist, community organizer and sex educator, passionate about sexual justice and gender equality and generally doing too many things at once.

www.ingramcontent.com/pod-product-compliance
Lightning Source LLC
Chambersburg PA
CBHW031322290526
45784CB00014B/622